Fidel Castro

Nick Caistor

REAKTION BOOKS

Published by Reaktion Books Ltd
33 Great Sutton Street
London EC1V ODX, UK

www.reaktionbooks.co.uk

First published 2013

Printed and bound in Great Britain
by Bell & Bain, Glasgow

British Library Cataloguing in Publication Data
Caistor, Nick.
    Fidel Castro. – (Critical lives)
    1. Castro, Fidel, 1926–
    2. Heads of state – Cuba – Biography.
    3. Cuba – Politics and government – 1959–1990.
    4. Cuba – Politics and government – 1990–
    I. Title II. Series
    972.9'1064'092-dc23

ISBN 978 1 78023 090 0

Contents

Preface

There is never any doubt when Fidel Castro Ruz is nearby. Over six feet tall, bulky and imposing, well-deserving of his nickname '*El Caballo*' (The Horse), with piercing light-blue eyes, he quickly becomes the centre of attention whether he is in a small room or a huge open-air space, such as Revolution Square in the centre of Havana, where he has made so many of his trademark hours-long speeches.

Fidel Castro not only brought revolution to Cuba, but went on to wield power there almost unchallenged for nearly fifty years, before ill health forced him to step down at the age of 81 in February 2008. The British historian Eric Hobsbawm described him as 'by far the most important figure in the whole history of Cuba so far. He's the only one who has turned Cuba into a global concept.'[1] As part of that global role, for several decades he was one of the most prominent leaders in the developing world, ensuring that Cuba's voice was heard on the most contentious international issues. To many people, this prominence was at best ambiguous, since Castro can also be seen as someone who helped to bring the world the closest it has ever come to nuclear conflict. In October 1962 the Soviet Union and the United States were only hours away from unleashing their nuclear arsenals against each other over the question of missiles the Soviets had placed in Cuba.

Castro has consistently divided opinion. For most of the million or so Cubans who have fled the island since his 1959 Revolution, he is a power-crazed dictator. To successive administrations in Washington, he has been an irritant, someone who enjoyed tweaking the nose of the 'empire'. This constant battling with a much more powerful neighbour has won him support not only in Cuba and in the rest of Latin America, but all round the world. He has always been quick to respond to events outside the island and give his trenchant opinion: so, for example, in the hours after the 9/11 attacks on the United States when President George W. Bush called for a concerted international effort to fight terrorism, Fidel Castro was quick to point out that this should include the 'terrorists' in Florida who frequently launched attacks against his regime and were regarded as 'heroes' in the United States.

Many people in Latin America and the developing world have also applauded Castro's stubborn attempts to resist the spread of capitalist ideas over the entire globe. Since the end of the 1980s and the collapse of the communist regimes in the Soviet Union and Eastern Europe, together with the general discrediting of the ideals they were meant to embody, there has been a renewed if sometimes morbid interest in how 'socialist' Cuba and its leader have managed to survive for so long. As one Latin American foreign minister joked: 'Castro and his Cuba should be kept as they are in a zoo, as unique exhibits no longer to be found anywhere in the wild'.

The eleven million Cubans who continue to live under his uniquely Cuban kind of socialism seem equally divided. People I have spoken to on the island may complain bitterly about shortages, the lack of personal and political freedom, and yet they still often show a grudging respect for 'the great leader'. Much of this support comes from a fascination with Castro as a public figure, capable of dominating international meetings with his dynamic personality, especially in his trademark lengthy speeches to vast audiences.

It remains to be seen what will happen in Cuba once Fidel Castro finally dies. For the moment, he has handed over power to his younger brother Raúl, who for so many years seemed to exist in his shadow – as Fidel himself once unkindly remarked: 'I don't know how much he has been harmed by being my brother; because when there is a tall tree, it always casts a little shade on the others.'[2]

Raúl seems to have adopted the old adage of changing a little in order to change nothing. He has surrounded himself with trusted allies, some of whom are the last survivors of those who fought in the guerrilla war of the 1950s that brought them to power. Some day soon, however, there must be at least a generational renewal in Cuban politics, even though the apocalyptic scenario that has been forecast by many exiles in Miami may not become reality. After Fidel Castro it may not be the deluge in Cuba, although there are likely to be quite a few tropical storms.

In his final days, no longer wielding that much power and able only to appear rarely in public, Fidel Castro has continued to give his opinion through blogs and articles rather than speeches, focusing now on anything and everything that catches his interest, from the injustices suffered by Cuban boxers at the Beijing Olympics, to the dangers of racism in the United States. He has also published a lengthy series of interviews with the title *My Life: A Spoken Autobiography* that gives his version of all he has lived through and achieved.[3]

This seems therefore a good moment to look back with a more critical eye on his life and to try to separate legend from facts, as far as these can be gleaned from one of the most closely guarded regimes in the world. I have reported on Cuba and Fidel Castro over some twenty years for the BBC and elsewhere. I have spoken to many of his closest associates, as well as some of his fiercest critics – including several people who have tried to assassinate him – in the United States.

As far back as 1953, when he was in the dock for attacking the army barracks at Moncada in an attempt to overthrow the Batista regime, Castro claimed that whatever the court's verdict, 'History will absolve me!' Although many historians eschew the study of individuals since history in their view obeys greater laws, Fidel Castro's defence plea cries out for a verdict on his achievements and failings. In the following study, bringing together personal details and a discussion of the ideas driving him on throughout his life, I hope to lay before readers enough evidence for them to be able to come to their own conclusion.

1

Down on the Farm

The region of Galicia in northwest Spain can seem like a natural paradise. Its hills are green and wooded, the frequent rains make the land fertile, and its rivers are wide and powerful. The often rugged coast is bathed by the waters of the Atlantic. But life in the Galician countryside has always been hard: much of the land belongs to large landowners, while small farmers have struggled for centuries to make a living for themselves and their families. Isolated from the centre of imperial power in Madrid and the south of Spain, distant from the Mediterranean and its trade routes, Galicia has always looked out to America, and the harsh conditions in the province have meant that hundreds of thousands of Galician men and women have throughout history ventured overseas in search of a better life. (So many emigrated to Argentina in the late nineteenth and early twentieth centuries that Spanish immigrants there are collectively known as *gallegos* – people from Galicia). Cuba too, as one of Spain's last colonies, was a magnet for Galician emigrants: some of them farmers; others, as in the case of Fidel Castro's father Angel, as recruits in the Spanish army.

So it was that in 1895 the seventeen-year-old Angel Castro y Argiz from Láncara in the province of Lugo enlisted in the ranks of the Spanish colonial army. In the extensive autobiographical inter- views he gave to Ignacio Ramonet, editor-in-chief of *Le Monde diplomatique* magazine in 2007, published in English under the title *My Life*, Fidel Castro gives a more ideologically correct version of why his father fought with the Spanish. According to him, Angel took the place of a rich Galician landowner, who paid him in order to avoid military service.[1] Castro admits however that he never discussed the matter with his father, while his sister Juanita always denied their father crossed the Atlantic as a Spanish soldier. In the mid-1890s, Spain was still clinging on to the few remaining colonies of an empire that had once stretched all round the globe. The last outposts were the Philippines in the Pacific, while Puerto Rico and Cuba were all that remained of Spain's once numerous possessions in the Americas. For centuries Cuba had been the regional centre of trade with Spain's peninsula: in the nineteenth century it continued to provide the mother country with sugar, tobacco, coffee and timber.

Spain's other colonies in Latin America had achieved independence early in the nineteenth century. In the Caribbean, the Dominican Republic became independent of Spain and Haiti in 1844. But Bolívar and the other heroes of the anti-Spanish campaigns on mainland Latin America considered Cuba a step too far, and it was left to home-grown independence fighters such as José Martí to organize the struggle to free themselves from the conservative Spanish elite ruling the island. The Cuban independence movement became increasingly active in the 1880s. By 1895 the Spanish government in Madrid recognized that the threat from the insurgents was so serious, that on the one hand they needed to step up their military presence on the island, and on the other to seek a long-lasting political solution. Angel Castro was probably among the 7,000 soldiers sent out under the new captain-general of the island, Arsenio Martínez-Campos, in April 1895. The new commander soon realized the extent of the problems facing him. By June 1895 he was writing to Madrid that 'my sincere and loyal opinion is that, with or without reforms, before twelve years we shall have another war'. Soon afterwards, he resigned his position, and the war he had predicted broke out twelve months rather than

Cuban troops in the War of Independence, 1898.

twelve years later.[2] The situation became even more complicated when the Spanish Prime Minister, Cánovas del Castillo, was assassinated in the Basque country in 1897, throwing Spain into political chaos. This gave the Cuban insurgents fresh impetus, but it was the entry into the conflict of a third, far more powerful, force that brought an end to nearly 500 years of Spanish colonial rule.

In January 1898 the battleship uss *Maine* was despatched to Havana to protect American citizens and business interests threatened by increasing turmoil on the island. On 15 February a massive explosion sank the vessel, with the loss of more than 260 lives. The Americans blamed the Spaniards, although the latter claimed that the sinking could only have been an on-board accident. Whatever the truth, the incident was enough to take the two countries to war. As was to happen some 65 years later when Fidel Castro himself was in power, the Americans began with a naval blockade of the island. This was quickly followed up by a land invasion. As a result, after a ten-week conflict, the u.s. forces achieved what the Cuban nationalists had been fighting to bring about for more than half a century: the departure of the Spaniards and the dismantling of their colonial rule.

Angel Castro was apparently stationed in the south of Cuba, but it is not clear if and when he was involved in the fighting against either the Cuban rebels or the American invaders. What is known is that he was one of thousands of conscripts sent back to Spain under the terms of the peace agreement signed in Paris in July 1898. Although the Americans occupied the island militarily for the next four years, they allowed the Spanish administrators and local government officials to stay on. They also encouraged the return of workers from northern Spain,[3] and Fidel's father seems to have been one of them, arriving back in Havana in December 1899.[4] At the dawn of the new century he began by working as a labourer for one of the companies brought in by the effective new rulers of the country: the Boston-based United Fruit Company. Angel was among the men employed to clear the native forests to make way for sugar cane plantations, probably on the 240,000 acres United Fruit purchased in the north of Oriente province, near Mayarí.[5] As stipulated in the Paris peace agreement, in 1902 the U.S. withdrew its occupying troops. Cuba was declared an 'independent republic', although still under the tutelage of the USA. Soon afterwards, Angel Castro bought a large tract of land near Birán, in the same Mayarí area. Whereas in Galicia he had struggled simply to survive, in Cuba he raised cattle, exploited the pine woods, and grew sugar cane on the Finca Manacas. With the thrift of a new immigrant, he soon became prosperous and gradually extended his house into a substantial raised building with room beneath it at night for cows, turkeys and other farm animals.[6] (The original farmhouse at Birán burned down in 1954 after Angel fell asleep holding a lit cigar, but after the 1959 Revolution a faithful replica was constructed, which now serves as a museum.)

By the end of the first decade of the twentieth century, Angel Castro felt sufficiently well-established to marry. He chose a bride, María Argota y Reyes, from another local Spanish family, and the couple were wed in March 1911. By 1918 they had five children, although only two survived beyond early childhood: Pedro Emilio and Lidia. By the mid-1920s, however, the marriage had foundered, and Angel took up with the family cook, Lina Ruz González, born in Cuba to a family originally from the Canary Islands and 28 years his junior. She was to bear him another seven children: Fidel was the third of these, born on 13 August 1926,[7] by which time his father was already in his fifties. It was not until 1941 that Angel finally became a Cuban citizen. He and Lina married in 1943, apparently after much cajoling by the devoutly Catholic Lina, now that divorce had been made legal under the terms of a new national constitution.

Fidel Castro has never had much to say about his relationship with his father. In 1985 he told the Brazilian priest Frei Betto that as a child he had never really talked with him about his past; from the brief comments he has made over the years, he gives the impression of regarding Angel as a very hard-working but inflexible and distant man, whom he respected but was in awe of. Others who knew Angel Castro have described him as a harsh man who talked little and preferred to give orders rather than explain himself. There is little suggestion that Angel was directly interested in politics, although his position as a landowner in Oriente province undoubtedly gave him considerable influence in local affairs. He appears to have had a peasant's strong attachment to working and owning land rather than being concerned about more abstract ideas such as 'nation' or political ideologies. Spanish-born, and with a wife of Spanish descent, he seems to have remained at a distance from native Cubans, while also showing little interest in the dramatic events unfolding in his home country in the 1920s and 1930s. Unlike Ernesto 'Che' Guevara's father in Argentina in

Lina Castro Ruz and Angel Castro, 1920s.

the second half of the 1930s, who was a strong supporter of the Spanish Republic, and welcomed Republican refugees to Córdoba in Argentina,[8] according to Fidel, his father was against the Republic, as were most of the other wealthy Spanish immigrants in Birán. Remembering this period in his lengthy interviews with Ignacio Ramonet in 2007, Castro is honest enough to admit that he himself had no political opinions when a boy, saying simply that 'All boys like war. Like everybody else, I also liked films, the Westerns, and what's more, I took them seriously'.[9]

Angel Castro found himself in an odd position, having left Cuba as part of a defeated army, but then returning as an ally of the new American masters. Over the years he became an influential figure in his own right, but his personal history meant he was doubly removed from the ordinary people of Cuba. On the one hand, he represented the colonial legacy of the Spaniards; while on the other he was closely identified not with the attempts to make Cuba properly independent, but more with the model proposed by the new colonial power. Some observers claim that his son's fight throughout his life for the independence of Cuba was born out of such contradictions.

People who knew the family well have commented that Fidel was his father's favourite, as he admired someone who showed a similar strength of character and stubbornness to his own. These neighbours from the Birán region also maintain that Fidel was the son who was closest in temperament to his father, and that while the two often argued, Angel perhaps felt proudest of his ambitious, tough offspring who was always ready to take on authority at school and at university. There are many possibly apocryphal stories of how the young Fidel is said to have fought against petty injustice, and he appears to have always been backed up by his father. Angel paid to give him a good education. He supported him throughout his years at university, and in the late 1940s is said to have bought him a new American car that quickly became used for political as well as romantic assignations. But when after university

Fidel began openly to oppose Fulgencio Batista's regime, he and his father appear to have had little to do with each other. Angel died at the age of 80 in 1956, when Fidel was living in exile in Mexico, frantically planning to return to Cuba and start a revolution.

Fidel has been less circumspect about his affection for his mother. He told Ignacio Ramonet:

> She was a cook, a doctor, a caretaker of all of us – she provided every single thing we might need, and she was a shoulder to cry on for any problem we might have. She didn't spoil us, though; she was a stickler for order, savings, cleanliness. She was the 'overseer', you might say, for all the daily tasks and routines inside and outside the house; she was the family economist. Nobody ever knew where she got the time and energy to do everything she did; she never sat down, I never saw her rest one second the whole day.[10]

If Angel Castro was distant, Fidel's mother Lina offered him warmth and security. Her beliefs were traditional, and central to them was her Catholic faith. In his 1985 interviews with the Brazilian theologian Frei Betto, Castro himself stressed this point:

> I would say that my mother's and my grandmother's religious beliefs were the result of family tradition. Both of them were very fervent believers. I remember that after the triumph of the revolution in 1959, I went to visit them in Havana. They were together, and my grandmother had some health problems. The room was full of saints and prayer cards. Throughout the struggle, which entailed great risks, both my mother and grandmother made all kinds of vows on behalf of our lives and safety.

He goes on to tell the Brazilian friar:

The infant Fidel in Birán, 1928.

I was very respectful of their beliefs. They told me about the vows they had made and their deep faith . . . I always listened to them with great interest and respect. Even though I did not share their view of the world, I never argued with them about these things, because I could see the strength, courage and comfort they got from their religious feelings and beliefs.[11]

It was Lina who insisted that Fidel and her other children by Angel should be baptized. It was for this ceremony at the age of five that Fidel was given this Christian name. He himself once told a journalist somewhat melodramatically: 'I had no name of my own. I was called Fidel because of somebody who was going to be my godfather' (Fidel Pino Santos – although in the end he never did become his godfather).[12] Instead it was the Haitian consul in Santiago de Cuba, married to the teacher where the young Fidel was lodged when first sent away to school there, who stepped in. Several writers have commented on the effect that being born 'out of wedlock' might have had on Fidel as a growing boy, speculating that this could have been one of the origins of his rebelliousness against the society in which he grew up. In his book *The Boys from Dolores*, Patrick Symmes argues that

> the rumour of their unconventional origins spread from the farm in Birán to the town of Banes, and followed them to Santiago. Out in the countryside of Oriente, even in a busy town like Banes, such casual family arrangements could be ignored, even tolerated. But in a big and pretentious city like Santiago, among boys from elite families with ancient Spanish surnames, legitimacy still had its prerogatives.[13]

One of the Jesuits who taught Fidel and his brother Raúl, Father Llorente, was even more outspoken:

> In Spain and Cuba they were too tough with these cases. So he hated society. He spoke to me about his mother not being the mother of the first two children of his father, and this was difficult and complicated for him.[14]

These two children were Fidel's half-brother Pedro Emilio, who stayed with his father after the divorce, and Lidia, who went with her mother. Pedro Emilio later became a poet, was regarded by many in his family as something of a wastrel, and was no great sympathizer of the Revolution. But Father Llorente's view is obviously coloured by his Catholicism. In the Cuban countryside very few couples bothered to make their unions official with either church or civil authorities. After his first marriage to Mirta Díaz-Balart, Fidel himself was not concerned whether his union with Dalia Soto was legalized or not. In this, as in much else, he appears to have inherited his father's attitude, rather than deliberately taking up an ideological position against marriage.

Regardless of the strains within this large and complicated family, his mother Lina remained close to Fidel and Raúl throughout her life. In August 1958, as the guerrilla war was reaching its climax, she smuggled a letter through to Fidel:

> Every day I pray to God that we will soon be able to hug, all of us together and full of joy, surrounded by LIBERTY that you love just as all Cubans. Every mother is proud of her children, even if her children are nothing more than just her children, but that is not the case with me, because in all of you I have more than just children. You are true heroes, the heroes of the youth and of the entire community that has their hope and faith in you. For this reason, I feel twice as proud of my sons . . .[15]

In 1959, after the victory of the Revolution, Lina went to Havana to see Fidel and Raúl enter the capital in triumph, but soon returned to Birán. She died at her daughter Juanita's home in the Havana suburb of Miramar in 1963.

Fidel had six full brothers and sisters. The eldest was Ramón, reputedly 'just like Fidel, only a peasant version'. He seems to have lacked the force of character of his younger brother, but as the eldest son took on the farm following his father's death. Ramón expressed his bitterness when his farm and landholdings were confiscated under the agrarian reform laws brought in by Fidel soon after the triumph of the Revolution, but later became involved with various agricultural projects suggested by his brother, including ambitious genetic experiments to improve the breeds of cattle on the island. Castro's elder sister Angela also lived most of her life out in the countryside, on a large farm in Capdevila on the outskirts of Havana. She died there aged 88 in February 2012.

Fidel had three younger sisters. Perhaps the best known of them is Juanita, who emigrated to Miami in 1964, where she ran a pharmacy for many years. She secured an exit visa from Cuba, claiming she wanted to go and stay with her sister Emma, who had been living in Mexico City since soon after the Revolution, but then went on to Miami and was to become one of her brother's most persistent critics. Like others in her family, Juanita was outraged at Fidel's refusal to treat his own family any differently when it came to the redistribution of land. One of his statements that she found most offensive was when, according to her, he described all family ties as being 'produced by virtue of animal instinct', which she interpreted as an insult to herself and the rest of the Castro family. The youngest of the siblings, Agustina, has stayed in Cuba, although her sons now live in Florida. In many ways, the Castro family is as divided as most Cuban households, with some of its members living on the island and others in the u.s., split by ideological but also economic necessities, and yet still retaining a strong sense of kinship.

As we shall see throughout this book, by far the most important relationship Fidel Castro has enjoyed within his family is the one with his younger brother Raúl (born 3 June 1931). During their childhood, Raúl seemed to have had little of his older brother's charisma. Raúl spent less than a year at the Jesuit college in Belén before being expelled (which perhaps had something to do with why, when he was made head of the armed forces after 1959, the college was closed down and turned into a military academy). He made little impression on his teachers at the La Salle school they both attended, and never succeeded in finishing any university studies.

Three brothers: Fidel, Raúl and Ramón at Dolores, 1941.

Both parents seem to have agreed that Fidel and Raúl should leave Birán at an early age and receive their education from the Jesuits who were then pre-eminent in teaching the rural middle classes in Cuba. From the age of six, Fidel was at school in the regional capital of Santiago, followed by the Colegio de Dolores, a Jesuit-run secondary school in the same city. At sixteen Fidel went to study and live in the capital, where he was a boarder at Havana's Colegio de Belén, one of the most prestigious schools, also run by Jesuits.

Looking back on his schooling more than 70 years later, Castro saw very clearly all the values they had transmitted:

> Undoubtedly my teachers, my Jesuit teachers, especially the Spanish Jesuits, who inculcated a strong sense of personal dignity – regardless of their political ideas – influenced me. Most Spaniards are endowed with a sense of personal honour, and it's very strong in the Jesuits. They valued character, rectitude, honesty, courage, and the ability to make sacrifices. Teachers definitely have an influence. The Jesuits clearly influenced me with their strict organization, their discipline and their values. They contributed to my development and influenced my sense of justice – which may have been quite rudimentary but was at least a starting point.[16]

At other times, Castro has criticized the dogmatism and strictness of his Jesuit teachers, but as throughout Latin America, their schools in Cuba were well known for their high academic standards and a belief in learning and the use of reason for its own sake.[17] There can be no doubt that despite his clashes with the Jesuits and their attempts to impose religion and authority on him, by the time Fidel left secondary school for university in Havana both his teachers and his family background had contributed to giving him a great sense of his own worth, as well as a lack of fear when expressing his own thoughts and opinions as forthrightly as possible. In 1945 he enrolled in the University of Havana to study law. Although he followed the courses seriously enough, his real intention was to use the opportunities given to him as a student leader in order to launch his own political career.

In 1992, at the age of 66, Fidel Castro travelled to Galicia for the first time, and visited his father's birthplace in Lárnaca. He was accompanied by the president of the Xunta de Galicia, the right-wing politician Manuel Fraga, a man who had been in power almost as long as Fidel. Despite coming from opposite ends of the political spectrum, the two men got on very well. It seemed that they appreciated in each other the Galician virtues of tenacity, resilience and an eye for an opportunity that they both had amply demonstrated throughout their lives, qualities they shared with perhaps the most famous son of Galicia, the Spanish dictator Francisco Franco.[18]

2

Defying the Dictator

At the University of Havana politics was often a dirty, violent business, as different factions fought for control. Castro soon acquired the reputation of always carrying a gun, and of being able to use it. His activities as a student leader gave rise to interest elsewhere: an FBI report that described him as a gangster out to impose his views by violent means. Another more sympathetic, not to say sycophantic, view of Fidel as student leader was given in an interview by Alfredo Guevara, who had the distinction of defeating Fidel in a poll to become one of the faculty's student representatives in 1947:

> I was struck by what a powerful personality he had, such a great presence. The women in the philosophy department compared him to a Greek statue. I simply felt his amazing strength. I felt he was like a volcano or a hurricane, but I had no idea then where this great force would take us.[1]

Despite the fact that Fidel Castro never liked to come second, the two men remained close friends and political allies. After the revolutionary victory in 1959, Alfredo Guevara played a key role in helping to draw up the country's new constitution and laws. He was later the founder of the highly influential Cuban Film Institute (ICAIC), and has remained a faithful ally of Fidel's over the past six decades.

In 1947 Fidel joined the newly formed Partido Revolucionario Cubano Ortodoxo (Cuban Orthodox Revolutionary Party). The

Castro as student leader, late 1940s.

'revolutionary' part of its title referred back to the 1930s insurrection, when Cubans united, with Havana students at the fore, to oust the dictator Machado.[2] Castro soon became head of their Radical Action group, made up of around 50 students and other young people who were already convinced that Cuba needed remedies more drastic than mere parliamentary reform. A year later, the Ortodoxo party was thrown into chaos when its leader, the charismatic Eduardo 'Eddy' Chibás, committed suicide while taking part in a radio programme. This confusion did not prevent Fidel from putting himself forward to stand as an Ortodoxo candidate for the elections scheduled to take place in 1952. His oratorical skills were developed quickly during the turbulent years he spent studying law. In his first recorded speech, to a student assembly in July 1947, Fidel was already calling for his audience to 'unmask the merchants who profit by the blood of martyrs', and denouncing 'tyranny' and those 'groups who use the reason of force and not the force of reason'.[3] At the time, it was the corrupt Grau government that he was lambasting. In another speech a few months later he calls for 'co-operation among different social groupings, creating the fighting unity of the people, so that they can win their true independence, their economic liberation, and their political freedom. The definitive emancipation of our nation is the fundamental aim of the university'.[4] It could be said that many of the key themes of Castro's political doctrine – independence, political and economic freedom, and true emancipation – were present (if only in embryonic form) in the 21-year-old's mind. There is already an enemy to be defeated thanks to 'unity', while in similar speeches from this period he is calling for 'revolution', although at this stage this has no great ideological import.

Even in his early twenties, Castro was looking beyond Cuba. As had become a tradition in Latin America since the nineteenth-century 'liberators' who fought to free the continent from Spanish rule, he saw efforts to free Cuba from neo-colonial dominion and dictatorship as part of a continent-wide struggle. He joined the Caribbean Legion, a group of democratically minded youngsters who underwent military training with the aim of deposing the dictator Rafael Trujillo in the nearby Dominican Republic, although in the end nothing came of their efforts. He was also part of a Cuban student delegation to Bogotá in 1948, and saw the power of mass protest when the inhabitants of the Colombian capital reacted with fury to the murder of the popular leader Jorge Eliecer Gaitán.

It was also in 1948 that Fidel married for the first time. His wife was Mirta Díaz-Balart, the daughter of a rich Havana family, whose father Lincoln was to become Batista's deputy interior minister. Their honeymoon, paid for by his in-laws, was the first time Fidel visited the United States. On 14 September 1949 came the birth of their first son, Fidelito.

Castro graduated with a law degree from Havana University in 1950. With two student colleagues, he set up a law practice in a poor district in the port of Havana, but as before his real interest lay in politics. He began actively campaigning around Havana for

Havana in the 1950s: a postcard printed in Chicago.

the Congressional elections planned for June 1952, taking every opportunity to criticize the corruption of the Carlos Prío regime. The parliamentary route was blocked when, on 10 March 1952, Fulgencio Batista, who had led a reformist government during the war years, seized power in a coup backed by the armed forces. Most of the opposition political parties, including the influential Communists in the Popular Socialist Party (PSP) dithered, not wanting to give up the hope of exerting influence on the Batista government. Fidel Castro was one of the few politicians to attack this takeover from the first. He was quick to publish a manifesto denouncing the coup and stating in no uncertain terms that it had no legitimacy beyond that of 'brute force overriding human reason'.[5]

By now, the main lines of his thought were already well defined. His analysis of Cuba and its political and social problems was in many ways akin to that of the great nineteenth-century patriot José Martí. This poet and political leader spent much of his life in exile in the United States, trying to bring together the warring factions who all claimed to want to hasten Cuban independence. Finally in 1892 Martí succeeded in uniting them in the Cuban Revolutionary

Party, after which in April 1895 he embarked on an invasion of the east of the island (Fidel Castro was plainly modelling himself on his predecessor when he landed in a similar way in December 1956). Unlike Castro however, Martí was killed within weeks of his arrival and the attempt failed. In January 1899, Cuba's independence from Spain was declared, although the distance between this and true independence is reflected by the fact that the future government of the island was discussed in Paris by representatives of the colonial power and the new power in the region, the United States, but without a single Cuban delegate being invited.

The experience of the following decades, with coups, corrupt governments and administrations which continued to take their orders from Washington, convinced the young Fidel that Cuba was still fighting for its independence as Martí had been doing almost a century earlier. Already he saw the primary cause as being the overwhelming influence of the United States and its interests on the island – even though he did not as yet condemn this as capitalist exploitation. It was from Martí that the youthful Fidel Castro learned the importance of unifying behind a common cause, and to accept that this cause could win out only through sacrifice and battles. Fidel Castro quickly came to identify glory and his own place in history as being bound up with the fight for national free-dom, whatever the cost. Where his views did not coincide with those of Martí lie in the latter's firmly held belief that the main aim was for the landless poor to overthrow the big landowners. He rejected Marxist ideas of the central role of the state in creating a new society as simply being the imposition of another master on the populace.

In a series of speeches and broadcasts, Castro denied that Batista was bringing freedom by his coup. He argued:

> your votes are in rifles, never in [the popular] will. With all that, you can win a military takeover but never clean elections. Your assault on government lacks the principles that give legitimacy.[6]

He returned to this idea of legitimacy when he tried to take the Batista regime to court as a lawyer, alleging they were nothing more than seditious 'mutineers'. He maintained that

It is not sufficient that the mutineers claim so facilely that revolution is the source of law, since instead of revolution, there is restoration; instead of progress and order, there is barbarism and brute force. There was no revolutionary program, theory, or declaration that preceded the coup. There were only politicians without the people, converted into assailants of power. Without a new conception of the state, of society, of the judicial order based on profound historical and philosophical principles, there will be no revolution that generates laws. [7]

This is Castro's first known attempt to justify the use of force to bring about the complete transformation of a society. He is well aware that any such revolution must represent the will of the 'people', even though at this stage he is not so concerned with the specifics of how their will is to be interpreted. In another article written during this period under a pseudonym that was published in the underground anti-Batista magazine *El Acusador*, Castro declares that he has a 'blind faith in the masses' and is convinced that the 'irreducible force of great ideas' will inevitably win out over tyranny.

It was not long before Castro moved against Batista. He began to organize and train other young activists from the Ortodoxo Party to take direct action against his regime. He could soon count on several hundred followers. Then on 26 July 1953 at the age of 26, he led a group of 160 young men and women in a failed attempt to take over the Moncada Barracks, the second largest in the country, in his old home of Santiago de Cuba. Never one to lack self-confidence, Castro had previously issued a manifesto in which he outlined the main aims of the revolutionary government he hoped to install:

> 1) The revolutionary government would return power to the people and restore the 1940 constitution; 2) land would be expropriated from large landowners and turned over to small-holders etc; 3) workers given rights to share 30% of profits of all large sugar, industrial, mercantile, and mining enterprises; 4) all sugar planters would have the right to share 55% of production; 5) wealth of those with 'ill-gotten gains' would be confiscated, and half of property recovered would go to workers – the other half to hospitals, asylums, orphanages.[8]

One of the people who was meant to see that this manifesto was published in the press and broadcast on the radio was the beautiful young socialite Naty Revuelta. A follower of the Ortodoxo party, she was also personally attracted to Fidel (and later had a daughter by him). According to her, the attack on the Moncada Barracks was neither foolhardy nor poorly planned. The barracks were chosen because they were thought to be one of the dictatorship's weak points – in addition, she says, the plan was to capture army weapons and then to head for the mountains in order to start a guerrilla campaign.[9] In her view then, as early as 1953 Fidel Castro was envisaging taking on the Batista regime militarily, and doing so from the countryside rather than the towns and cities.

These appeals to the populace in general were meant to coincide with a popular uprising in the city of Santiago, but this never materialized. Castro and his followers were quickly repulsed from the Barracks. In the ensuing persecution, as many as 60 of the attackers were killed or tortured. Fidel and his brother Raúl succeeded in avoiding immediate capture, and thanks to the intervention of the local Catholic bishop, their lives were spared.

On 21 September 1953 Fidel was put on trial along with another 100 defendants, accused under Article 148 of the country's penal code of 'leading an attempt aimed at organizing an uprising of armed persons against constitutional powers of the state'.[10]

Although at the outset the judges allowed Fidel Castro to conduct his own defence, by the end of the fifth day of the trial the court falsely announced that he was too sick to continue. It was not until mid-October (by which time his brother Raúl and 28 others had been found guilty) that the charges were brought against Fidel himself – in the local hospital. When Fidel finally did get to present his defence, he gave a bravura performance, the first of many that were to follow over the next five decades. He used the opportunity to deliver a stinging attack on the legitimacy of the Batista regime, claiming that 'the only remedy against force without authority is to oppose it with force'. He once again defended the legitimacy of revolutionary action if it was undertaken against a tyrannical government. He insisted that 'the revolutionary movement, as the momentary incarnation of that sovereignty which is the only source of legitimate power, would assume all the faculties inherent in sovereignty, such as the power to legislate, to enforce laws, and to judge', concluding that 'a government acclaimed by the mass of combatants would receive and be vested with the necessary power to proceed to establish effectively the will of the people and true justice'.[11] His defence ended with what was to become one of his most famous phrases: '*La historia me absolverá*' (History will absolve me!).[12] More than 40 years later, Fidel himself provided a further commentary on this famous declaration. In his interviews with the veteran Nicaraguan Sandinista guerrilla leader Tomás Borge, the Cuban leader commented:

That was an expression of confidence in the ideas I was defending as the fairest ones, and of the cause I was defending as the most honourable one. I meant that the future would recognise this because, in the future, those ideas would be made realities; in the future, people would know everything about what had happened, what we did and what our adversaries did, what goals we sought and what goals our adversaries sought, and who was right – we or the judges who were trying us, who had acted dishonestly in discharging a public trust, who had abandoned their oath of loyalty to the Constitution, and were serving a tyrannical regime. I was challenging them, absolutely convinced that the ideas we were defending would triumph in our homeland some day – a conviction I still have, that humanity's legitimate causes will always advance and eventually triumph.[13]

In an attempt to prevent Fidel from gaining any further political advantage out of the trial, the proceedings against him were rushed through in only a few hours. Found guilty, he was sentenced to fifteen years' imprisonment and sent to the Isla de Pinos, south of the mainland. When he arrived on the island, he set out almost at once to organize what he grandly termed the 'Abel Santamaría Ideological Academy' (named after one of his fellow attackers of the Moncada Barracks, who was captured and tortured to death). This was intended to offer a wide range of educational opportunities to his fellow inmates, from learning to read and write to discussions on history and politics. The prison authorities were surprisingly liberal, allowing Fidel and the others to receive many books. According to Naty Revuelta, it was also here that he began a thorough study of Marxist texts, which she smuggled in for him. To Castro, these months provided him with a golden opportunity to study and think. As he wrote in a letter from prison:

What a fantastic school this prison is! Here, I have forged my vision of the world and have found the meaning of my life. Will it be long or short? I do not know. Fruitful or sterile? But there is something I feel reaffirming itself within me; my passionate desire to sacrifice and struggle.[14]

In prison he was also busy continuing to organize his supporters on the outside, in what now became known as the *Movimiento 26 de Julio* (26th of July Movement) in honour of the failed attack. These efforts were interrupted in mid-April 1954, when he was punished with solitary detention after the prisoners had sung the newly penned anthem of the 26th of July Movement during a visit by the dictator Fulgencio Batista. Even so, outside the prison some ten thousand copies of Fidel's 'History Will Absolve Me!' speech were printed and distributed throughout Cuba. In this way his name and reputation as one of the leading opponents against an increasingly oppressive regime remained present in the minds of the Cuban population.

Another less public but more personally revealing publication from Castro's prison days are the letters he wrote to his former wife Mirta Diaz-Balart, to his half-sister Lidia, to a future mistress, and to his close ally Luis Conte Agüero. It was Agüero who had the 21 letters published in Havana shortly after the victory of the Revolution in 1959, although he lost faith in the direction in which his erstwhile friend was leading the country, and like so many thousands of his countrymen he soon decamped to Miami. Because of this, the book was withdrawn from circulation inside Cuba, and only surfaced again in English translation in 2007.

The almost religious fervour of Castro's Moncada Barracks defence speech is taken up again in a letter to the father of one of the combatants who fell in the attack:

I will not speak of him as if he were absent, he has not been and he will never be. These are not mere words of consolation. Only those of us who feel it truly and permanently in the depths of our souls can comprehend this. Physical life is ephemeral, it passes inexorably. . . This truth should be taught to every human being – that the immortal values of the spirit are above physical life. What sense does life have without these values? What then is it to live? Those who understand this and generously sacrifice their physical life for the sake of good and justice – how can they die? God is the supreme idea of goodness and justice. Those who fall for these causes on the soil of the motherland will go to God.[15]

Many of the letters concern more personal matters. His first wife, Mirta Diaz-Balart, had left the island in 1954 with their son Fidelito after she discovered that Fidel had been having a prolonged affair with Naty Revuelta. From inside his cell, Fidel wrote to his sister Lidia in terms which show that the battle for custody of his son could bring out equally grandiloquent protests as his political beliefs:

I do not care one bit if this battle drags on till the end of the world. If they think they can exhaust my patience and, based on this, that I am going to concede – they are going to find that I am wrapped in Buddhist tranquillity and am prepared to re-enact the famous Hundred Years War – and win it! To these private matters, add my reflection on the political panorama – and it will not be difficult to imagine that I will leave this prison as the man of iron.[16]

Taken as a whole, the prison letters show traits in the young revolutionary that seem only to have become more pronounced with age: the self-righteous anger; the insistence on honour and dignity; the sheer boundless confidence not only in himself but in the fact that he will win, whatever the odds stacked against him – in fact, the more difficult the challenge, the better. At the same time, they suggest that even before seizing power, the ability to

Castro released from the Isla de Pinos, May 1955.

see the other person's point of view, still less to compromise in any way, was dismissed as unnecessary, a sign of weakness.

On 15 May 1955, Fidel, his brother Raúl and the other political detainees on the Isla de Pinos strolled out of the prison. A photographer was on hand to capture the moment, and his image shows Fidel in the exact centre of the emerging group, his right arm raised in defiant greeting. He is the only one of the prisoners not carrying a suitcase – it seems that his brother Raúl, on his far right, is the one delegated to do that. The prisoners benefited from a general amnesty decreed by Batista, who apparently was attempting to improve his image internationally, particularly in the United States.

Although Fidel at first hoped he would be able to continue his political activities on the island, he soon realized this would be too dangerous. He quickly came to suspect that the release had been a trap set by Batista. A few weeks later, as if to confirm his suspicions, his brother Raúl was accused of planting a bomb in a Havana cinema. He sought asylum in the Mexican embassy, and soon left for Mexico City and exile. Fidel stayed on, reviving his links with the grass-roots members of the Ortodoxo party, and with other opponents of Batista such as Frank País, who, like Fidel, was the son of immigrants from Galicia, and by now one of the leaders of the urban wing of the 26th of July Movement in Santiago de Cuba.

In July 1955, Fidel followed his brother into exile in Mexico. As ever making the most of the occasion to publicize his actions, Fidel gave a defiant farewell speech to reporters at Havana airport:

> I am leaving Cuba because all doors of peaceful struggle have been closed to me. Six weeks after being released from prison I am convinced more than ever of the dictatorship's intention, masked in different ways, to remain in power for twenty years, ruling as now by the use of terror and crime and ignoring the patience of the Cuban people, which has its limits. As a follower of Martí, I believe the hour has come to take our rights and not to beg for them, to fight instead of pleading for them. I will reside somewhere in the Caribbean. From trips such as this, one does not return, or else one returns with the tyranny beheaded at one's feet.[17]

Raúl had already been active in recruiting sympathizers for their cause in the Mexican capital. In July 1955 he introduced his brother to a young Argentine firebrand, Ernesto 'Che' Guevara. Ever since the Mexican Revolution and the left-wing nationalist governments of the 1930s, the Mexican authorities had been surprisingly open to revolutionaries from other countries. Leon Trotsky had gone there in the late 1930s when he could find no safe haven in Europe (although Mexico was to prove even less safe for him in the end). Thousands of Republican exiles from the Spanish Civil War also flocked to Mexico, providing a new intellectual, cultural and political ferment. In the 1950s, although Mexico's internal politics under the increasingly authoritarian PRI (Institutional Revolutionary Party) was increasingly authoritarian and intolerant of dissent, foreign policy was still progressive, particularly with regard to Latin America and the Caribbean. Political refugees from the Dominican Republic as well as Cuba, Venezuela, Peru and the Central American republics were relatively free to congregate, debate and plot in Mexico City and elsewhere.

One of those drawn to Mexico in this way was the young doctor and would-be revolutionary Ernesto Guevara de la Serna. Although he had scarcely been involved in politics in his own country during his middle-class upbringing, several trips through South America had convinced him of the malign influence of the United States and capitalism in general, and of the need for popular revolution to put an end to the glaring social inequalities he had witnessed. His convictions were reinforced by his 1954 experiences in Guatemala, where he saw how a left-wing reformist government under President Jacobo Árbenz was first undermined and then overthrown by a CIA-backed military coup. Guevara thought that the president had been wrong not to arm his supporters to fight back against the military, and had no qualms about the use of violence to achieve political goals aimed at creating social justice and greater national sovereignty.

When he reached Mexico in October 1954, however, the 26-year-old Guevara had little idea of where exactly he should take the fight to in order to advance these ideals. Through Cuban exiles he had first met in Guatemala, he soon fell in with Raúl Castro and other opponents of the Batista regime in Cuba. Guevara was one of the first people Raúl encouraged Fidel to meet. After being introduced at the flat belonging to an affable Cuban woman, María Antonia González, and her partner, a Mexican boxer, the two men continued their conversation at a restaurant. According to the official Cuban version of this encounter, they were immediately on the same wavelength, and Guevara at once signed up for his new

Cuban friend's ambitious scheme to return at the head of an invasion force. The Argentine was sufficiently impressed to write in his diary:

> One political event is to have met Fidel Castro, the Cuban revolutionary, an intelligent young man who is very sure of himself and very audacious; I think we both liked each other.[18]

Over the months that followed, their friendship deepened, and as the small band of Cuban exiles trained, collected funds and made plans for the overthrow of the Batista regime, Fidel was soon aware that his Argentine friend's talents went far beyond his medical training. On one occasion he even criticized his Cuban colleagues for tiring too easily, holding up the person they had by now christened as 'Che' (a common Argentine term for 'man' or 'guy') as an example to the rest of them. Fidel also put Guevara in charge of discipline among the would-be fighters, even though some of them resented taking orders from a non-Cuban. Guevara's experience of growing up in towns and cities of the prosperous Argentina of the 1930s and 1940s was very different to that of Fidel Castro in the Cuban provinces, but they both shared the passionate belief that revolutionary change in Latin America was necessary and possible, and that they were predestined to play an important role in bringing this about. As well as making sure his men were trained in the use of weapons (a veteran colonel from the Spanish Civil War was their chief trainer), Fidel toured the United States to raise funds. In Miami's Flagler Theatre he made an impassioned plea for help, arguing that 'revolutions are based on morals. A movement that has to rob banks or accept money from thieves cannot be considered revolutionary'. His appeals for money from the Cuban opponents to Batista in the United States were successful enough for him to buy weapons and a motor cruiser that was to play a vital part in his plans.

Fidel was in a hurry to return to Cuba. 'In 1956 we will be free or we will be martyrs', he told his followers. Part of his haste was because he did not want any other political groups to take the lead in the struggle against Batista and leave him on the sidelines. He declared his distance from the leadership of the Ortodoxo party, defining his group as the 'vanguard' of the resistance to the tyranny. In mid-1956 his plans almost came to nothing when the Mexican authorities arrested him, driving a car with a boot full of weapons. Che and many of the other Cuban exiles were picked up soon afterwards and held in the Interior Ministry jail. Most of the men were released over the following days, but Che, Fidel and another Cuban were kept in prison for several weeks. The three were finally set free at the end of July 1956, after Fidel paid a fine (and a bribe) to the Mexican police, and promised that he would soon be leaving the country.

This close attention from the Mexican police had indeed made Fidel even more determined to leave for Cuba as quickly as possible. He continued to train his men, and methodically chose 80 or so of those he most trusted to accompany him on the leaky motor launch *Granma* in late November 1956. Guevara was one of the first on his list – although just how good a doctor the Argentine was is debatable, as he forgot both his asthma inhalers and the seasick pills that would have made a huge difference to the novice sailors when their vessel struggled through storms and heavy seas towards the island. Fidel Castro set out to take the fight to Batista despite the fact that the 26th of July Movement on the island and other organized anti-Batista groups all urged him to postpone the risky adventure. As Sebastian Balfour puts it:

Castro's decision to go ahead with the mission illustrated once again his belief in the overriding importance of public relations and his voluntarist faith in the triumph of will over logistics.[19]

As the Batista regime grew increasingly repressive, and the opposition better organized and with greater popular support, Fidel did not want the glory of toppling the dictator to be snatched by someone else.

3

Making the Revolution

In the early hours of 26 November 1956 the would-be liberators set off from the port of Tuxpán on Mexico's Caribbean coast. Fidel was accompanied aboard the motor launch *Granma* by his brother Raúl, Che Guevara and 79 others as they sailed through stormy weather across the Gulf of Mexico back towards Cuba. The plan was to land in the east of the island and link up with popular insurrections planned to take place in Santiago de Cuba and other major cities, but the crossing and the landing proved an almost complete disaster. The *Granma*'s engine failed, they got lost at sea, and when they eventually made land in Cuba it was in the wrong place, in the middle of an inhospitable mangrove swamp. The popular uprisings were easily snuffed out before the *Granma* fighters arrived, and the two groups of survivors from the *Granma* failed to link up on shore. Worse still, their position had been given away to the Batista forces, and within a few days of landing, Fidel and his followers were almost wiped out. It was not until the middle of December that the remaining twenty or so fighters – including Raúl and Che – met up again in the mountains of the Sierra Maestra. And yet the French writer and philosopher Jean-Paul Sartre, who visited Cuba in 1960 a few months after the guerrilla victory, could look back on those first difficult days with a novelist's imaginative eye and see them as the moment when everything changed in Cuba:

And then came one day, which promised to be neither better nor worse than all the others. In Havana that morning, as every morning, the police toured the gambling houses and collected the chief's commission; the morals squad fleeced the girls. The newspapers spoke of Wall Street and of the social set – who was at whose house last evening. They published the list of the most celebrated hosts in Cuba. The sky was cloudy, a strong breeze; maximum temperature 82 degrees in the west, in the east 86 degrees or a little more. It was December 2, 1956. On that day, without warning, the revolution began.[1]

Despite the near disaster, it was not long before Fidel was optimistic once more about the chances of overthrowing Batista. As well as setting up camp for the guerrillas high in the mountains, he made contact with the 26th of July Movement activists in Havana and the east of the island. Together with them, he published a new manifesto. In it, the signatories stressed that the revolution they intended to usher in would not owe anything to previous ones, but would be specific to the time and place in which it was created: 'the ideology of the Cuban Revolution must arise from its own roots and the particular circumstances of the people and the country.' At that moment in time Castro needed above all to win as much support as possible, and not to tie the Revolution to any set ideology, Marxist or otherwise.

The small guerrilla army began to make forays out of its Sierra Maestra stronghold to harass army and police posts, and to gather weapons and new recruits. In addition to his military and political endeavours, Fidel appreciated the importance of generating news that could be used for propaganda purposes, especially since the Batista press had boasted of his death during the botched landing. Castro not only set up a rebel radio station and a printing press, but offered interviews to any reporters willing to make the long and dangerous trek up into the Sierra Maestra. By far the most important of these internationally was the 17 February 1957 interview with Herbert Matthews from *The New York Times*, published a week later. In his report, Matthews refuted the Batista government's propaganda that Castro had been killed and his movement wiped out, and wrote that Castro 'has strong ideas of liberty, democracy, social justice, the need to restore the constitution, to hold elections'. He also described Castro as 'anti-communist' and was clearly impressed:

> the personality of the man is overpowering. It was easy to see that his men adored him and also to see why he has caught the imagination of the youth of Cuba all over the island. Here was an educated, dedicated fanatic, a man of ideals, of courage and of remarkable qualities of leadership.

Little wonder that Castro's lieutenant Che said of Matthews's articles that they were 'far more important than any military victory.'[2]

Throughout 1957 Castro and his forces consolidated their position in the Sierra Maestra. At the same time, by sharing the

A primitive armoured car from the early days of the uprising.

Relaxing with Celia Sánchez in the Sierra Maestra.

harsh conditions in the mountains that were daily life for the local farmers and landless peasants, Castro and his men sought to win hearts and minds, and to convince the local population that they understood how repression could destroy lives and hope. Many of the peasants were employed seasonally on the plantations and faced half a year with little or no work. According to some estimates, as many as a third of them were illiterate, and had never been to school. Although some locals remained suspicious of the *barbudos*, 'bearded ones', Castro was extremely successful in persuading many of the surrounding population that they shared a common enemy, and that they should stand together. In this way, the guerrilla forces grew quickly, their numbers swelled by locals who for years had suffered violence at the hands of the army or landowners, long before the arrival of the guerrilla band. Another important new recruit was Celia Sánchez. A doctor's daughter from the town of Manzanillo in Oriente province, her militant Catholicism first persuaded her to oppose the Batista regime. The attack on the

Moncada Barracks led her to join the 26th of July Movement, and she first made contact with the tiny rebel army in December 1956, acting as a liaison between them and Frank País and the resistance in the east of the island. A few months later, she went up into the Sierra Maestra to stay, soon becoming Fidel's most trusted aide. While he was the one who planned strategy and the political future, she was the person who sorted out the day-to-day details. She looked after his health, filtered the people who wanted to meet him and made sure the rebel fighters maintained good relations with the peasant farmers in the region. She joined in the final assault in December 1958, and entered Havana with Fidel. After the revolutionary victory, her small apartment on Calle 11 in Havana's Vedado district was the second, unofficial centre of the revolutionary government. Officials as well as ordinary Cubans knew that to get to see Fidel they had first to go through Sánchez. According to Alfredo Guevara, quoted by Ann Louise Bardach:

> She kept Fidel in touch with the people. She was a thousand times more effective than any intelligence organization and she was one of the few people who could tell Fidel news he didn't want to hear.[3]

By mid-1958, the military and political balance had turned decisively in favour of the guerrilla group. As a military commander, Fidel proved himself to be a master strategist, leading small groups to attack army units, and then pulling back and vanishing before greater numbers of reinforcements or air support could turn the situation to the regular army's advantage. Although they greatly outnumbered the insurgents, the government forces had little experience of fighting in mountains with dense jungle undergrowth, and were also undermined by internal rivalries. Early in the year, the guerrillas succeeded in driving back a determined army offensive, and by September Castro felt able to send two columns of about 100 men each out of the Sierra to spread the fight further west. These columns were led by Che Guevara and Camilo Cienfuegos. Cienfuegos was to march with his men to the west of Havana and Pinar del Río province, while Che was ordered to take the fight to the Las Villas province and the Escambray mountains in the centre. Castro considered it important that a separate guerrilla group already operating there under the command of Eloy Gutiérrez Menoyo be brought under his control. The strategic aim of the guerrillas was to cut Havana off from the eastern end of the island so that no more reinforcements could be sent.

After the near disaster of the landing on the southeast coast of Cuba, Guevara had soon taken on a military as well as a medical role. He has described his 'Damascene moment' when instead of rescuing a knapsack full of medicines he chose to pick up a rifle,[4] and it was not long before Fidel recognized his qualities as a military leader and tactician. By July 1957 he made the Argentine a *comandante* in the rebel army, appointing him his second-in-command over his own brother Raúl and all the other Cubans, many of whom were older and more experienced than he was. At the same time, Fidel carefully kept the Argentine out of any direct political role, especially following the 1957 murder of Frank País, the leader of the 26th of July Movement in Santiago de Cuba. As a foreigner, Guevara would probably only have created more divisions in an already fragmented organisation. Fidel also deliberately chose Guevara as the person who dispensed revolutionary justice among the guerrilla fighters: in part because as he has always insisted, he saw the Argentine as someone who had great moral authority and was a 'model for the revolutionary man', also no doubt to keep his own hands as clean as possible.

Fidel did however consider his Argentine colleague as being too willing to put himself in the front line and risk being killed. In *My Life* he says bluntly: 'Che wouldn't have come out of that war alive if some control hadn't been put on his daring and his tendency towards foolhardiness.'[5] When he chose him to lead one of the columns that took the guerrilla war out of the Sierra Maestra to the rest of the island, he also made it plain to Guevara that he was not to put himself at personal risk.

The increasing military pressure from Castro's guerrilla forces contrasted with the relative failure of the general strike called on 9 April 1958 by the leaders of the 26th of July Movement in the *llano*, the territory outside the sierra. Although the original idea had been to combine the rural guerrilla with strikes, sabotage and other resistance in Cuba's towns and cities involving organized workers' groups, the impact of the successful struggle in the Sierra Maestra led to it becoming the centre of opposition to Batista, with Castro at its head. In July 1958 he issued a second manifesto, once more calling for revolutionary change, agrarian reform and the restoration of constitutional rights, but with a few more specific indications of the direction in which he hoped to take Cuba after the guerrilla victory. By now, even the Communist Party of Cuba (known as the Popular Socialist Party or PSP) was willing to come and meet him for talks. Founded in 1925, the Communist Party of Cuba had a long tradition of successful organization among the working class, especially in the more developed areas of Havana and towns in the west of the island, although its reputation was somewhat tarnished because it had joined Batista's government during his first, legitimate period in office in the 1940s. In keeping with the traditional Marxist line as promoted by Moscow, the PSP's leaders believed that any revolution in Cuba would necessarily be led by the urban industrial workers. Consequently, the party had initially been dismissive of the guerrilla effort in the remote countryside, and suspicious of Fidel as the leader of efforts to topple Batista. However, by late 1958, the PSP had come to recognize his central importance, although it still apparently believed that it could play the most important role in creating the revolutionary society to come after the removal of the dictator.

The first revolutionary column reaches Havana, January 1959.

The final push to overthrow Batista began in November 1958. Fidel and Raúl closed in on Santiago de Cuba, while the other two columns effectively cut Havana off from the east of the island. After a surprisingly short final push, the guerrillas seized the towns and cities in the east and west of the island. In Havana there were strikes and acts of open opposition to the regime. On New Year's Eve 1958, Batista fled to the neighbouring Dominican Republic and a welcome from its dictator Rafael Trujillo. He left behind a military junta, but this collapsed within a matter of hours. By 2 January 1959, guerrilla forces under Camilo Cienfuegos and Che Guevara moved into the capital and took control, while Castro himself remained in Santiago de Cuba. Over the following days, he made his way overland to the capital with deliberate slowness, building up the sense of expectation before his arrival with his usual astute stage management. He finally reached Havana on 8 January 1959. Naty Revuelta, who had been one his lovers in the early 1950s and was the mother of his eldest daughter, remembered those days:

It was incredible. In the thousand kilometres from Oriente to Havana, the entire island went to the central highway to cheer and throw flowers, to see the *barbudos* [the bearded guerrilla fighters]. It was surprising the island didn't sink. That lasted for eight days, and everybody was really on the streets.[6]

In the first of hundreds of lengthy speeches to huge crowds, Fidel used what became a common rhetorical device, asking the people in front of him questions, and then claiming he was only doing their will based on their answers. He ended by asserting, in the early hours of the next morning:

For us, principles are above all other considerations, and we do not struggle because of personal ambition. I believe we have demonstrated sufficiently that we have fought without personal ambition. I believe no Cuban can have the slightest doubt of that![7]

Over the coming decades, this was precisely the doubt that came to preoccupy many people both within Cuba and outside the island.

Fidel Castro's forces came to power exactly 60 years after the Spaniards had relinquished control over the island to the new colonial power, the United States. As usual with someone so obsessed with history and its lessons, the significance of this date was not lost on Fidel. In his first speech on national radio from Santiago de Cuba on 2 January 1959, he promised that this time around there would be real independence for all Cubans:

This time, luckily for Cuba, the Revolution will truly arrive at its goal. It will not be like '98, when the Americans came in and made themselves the owners here. It will not be like '33, when the people began to believe a revolution was in the making and Batista came and betrayed it, took power, and installed a ferocious dictatorship. It will not be like '44, when the multitudes ardently believed that at last the people had taken power, but those who had taken over were the crooks. Neither crooks, nor traitors, nor interventionists. This time, yes, it is a Revolution![8]

However, although the war against the Batista regime had been won, the triumphant guerrillas now had to set about learning how to govern an entire country (then a nation of 6.5 million people). Castro could only be certain of unswerving support from the relatively small number of men and women who had fought the guerrilla campaign alongside him. The leaders and supporters of the political groupings in the country still had to be won over, as did the masses. In addition, Fidel had to quickly convince the inhabitants of Havana (where almost a third of the island population lived) that the Revolution had also been made on their behalf. As soon as he was installed in the capital, he attempted to do this by slashing urban rents by decree, and then forcing the American-run utility companies to reduce their tariffs. When both blue- and white-collar workers went on strike for more pay and benefits, the Revolutionary government supported them against the foreign-owned companies.

One of the most urgent questions facing the victorious guerrillas was how to bring in revolutionary change without resorting to more violence now that they were in power. As early as 1953, during his trial for the failed attack on the Moncada Barracks, Fidel had sought to emphasize the difference between what he argued was the bloodthirsty Batista regime (responsible apart from anything else for the torture and unlawful killing of more than 60 of those who had taken part in the assault) and the conduct of the men under his command:

Everyone had instructions, first of all to be humane in the struggle. Never was a group of armed men more generous to the adversary.

From the beginning we took numerous prisoners . . . Those
soldiers testified before the court, and without exception they
all acknowledged that we treated them with absolute respect . . . [9]

Time and again after that, Fidel emphasized the theme of
revolutionary purity versus the illegitimate and unprincipled
status quo. In the guerrilla struggle from 1956 to 1959, Castro had
seen how crucial it was for his fighters to ensure that they behaved
in a much more humane way than the security forces. In the mountains, alleged informers were executed after a brief trial, and so
were people who deserted from the rebel columns. But Castro's
main aim was to win over the landless peasants and their families
in the Sierra Maestra, in order to gain recruits for his own side and
help prevent them from betraying the guerrillas to the police or
army. In this context, it was sensible for him to insist that his
forces behave more fairly towards the population as a whole. He,
Che and the other *comandantes* knew that the more successful they
were, the more Batista's men would resort to terror, and thus drive
the peasants actively to support them. This humane attitude also
helped contradict the government propaganda that sought to
portray the guerrillas as a gang of outlaws or desperadoes who
were doing nothing more than stealing and committing other
common crimes.

The determination to seize the moral high ground also extended
to the treatment of captured soldiers and officers. As Castro wrote
in 1958:

With the legitimate pride of those who have known how to follow
and ethical norm, we can say that without one exception the
fighters of the rebel army have honoured their law with the
prisoners. Never did a prisoner forfeit his life, and never was a
wounded man left unattended. But we can say more: never was
a prisoner beaten. And further: Never was a prisoner insulted

or offended. All officers who were our prisoners can verify that no one was submitted to interrogation due to our respect of their condition as men and soldiers. The victories achieved by our troops without murdering, torturing, and even without interrogating the enemy demonstrate that abuse to human dignity can never be justified.[10]

This same approach prevailed in the final offensive against the Batista forces from November 1958 onwards. However, once Castro's rebels had won power, the situation was more delicate. What was to be done with members of the Batista armed forces and the police who had tortured and killed hundreds, if not thousands, of innocent Cubans in their efforts to hold on to power? What about the corrupt politicians who had stolen government funds? What about landowners who had abused the peasants for decades?

The answer that the newly victorious rebel leaders came up with led to one of the episodes that Castro's opponents have been quick to use against him ever since. The trials of those accused of abuses were held in public, and frequently shown live on state television. After what were often no more than summary proceedings, those found guilty were taken out and shot. Those mainly responsible for these executions were Che Guevara, who had been put in command of the new armed forces, and Castro's brother Raúl. There is no exact figure on the number of people executed in this way, although most commentators agree several hundred Batista supporters were killed during the first weeks of the Revolution. Recalling these events almost 50 years later in *My Life*, Fidel recognized that this had been a mistake:

I think the error may have been in the manner, shall we say, that those trials were conducted, using public places and allowing the proceedings to be attended by a great number of our country-men who were justly outraged by the thousands of crimes that had been committed. That might be in conflict, and in fact was in conflict, with our own ideas of justice. And it was very much exploited by the United States. We lost no time in rectifying what was unquestionably a mistake. But those guilty of genocide were tried and punished according to laws that had been passed long before by the Revolution, during the war.[11]

Eventually it was Fidel himself who put a stop to the trials being held in the Havana baseball stadium in the centre of the city, and who also stopped them being televised. Apart from this 'mistake', however, there was no mass bloodletting of supporters of the Batista regime. The fledgling new revolutionary army and police were able to prevent any widespread breakdown of law and order. In part this was because many of the worst human rights abusers immediately took flight for Miami, the Dominican Republic or other safe havens. In addition, the revolutionary government's intelligent management of the situation also helped: soldiers and officers from the old armed forces were offered the choice of joining the new rebel army, and many of them quickly accepted. Once they became part of the new security apparatus system, they were treated professionally and given the chance to succeed in their new roles.

During his exile in Mexico, and then in the two years fighting in the Sierra Maestra, it was the guerrillas, people willing to fight and risk their lives for their political beliefs, whom Castro saw as the essential element for building the revolutionary society. This insistence on the primacy of military values such as obeying orders, loyalty, comradeship, and courage over the more nuanced values of political debate and action remained a constant in Fidel Castro's thought. In spite of this belief, after the rebel victory he made strenuous efforts to broaden the base of his government. He wooed the 26th of July Movement by appointing Manuel Urrutia, who had been a judge opposed to Batista and had been forced into exile, as the first post-revolutionary president. Castro himself took the position of commander-in-chief of the armed forces, supplemented on 16 February by his appointment as prime minister in the revolutionary government. However, Urrutia was only to remain in office for a few months; by mid-1960 it had become clear that all real power was exercised by Fidel and a group of his closest associates: Raúl, Che Guevara and a handful of others, who met under the title of the 'Office for Revolutionary Planning and Co-ordination'. They were the ones who worked on the new revolutionary constitution and on planning the main radical changes that Castro saw as necessary.

On 17 May 1959, the long-promised land reform decree was published. Foreigners no longer had the right to buy land in Cuba. The big estates or *latifundias* were dissolved: no one was to own more than 400 hectares. This included Castro's own family: his father's estate in Birán was broken up, much to the indignation of his brothers and sisters, who could not swallow the revolutionary puritanism applied to their own family. The state took over unproductive land, and prepared to distribute it to landless peasants. The text of the agrarian reform decree clearly speaks of the need to increase agricultural production and to 'satisfy the food needs of the nation' as well as developing the internal market by 'raising the purchasing power of the rural population'. The reform was clearly intended to not only reduce the island's dependency on growing sugar for export, but also to increase employment in the countryside. In 1963, when the private farmers who still owned 400 hectares of land became increasingly hostile to the new government, a second Agrarian Reform Law was passed. This reduced the maximum private landholding to only 67 hectares. As a result, by the mid-1960s roughly 85 per cent of agricultural land in Cuba was owned by the state compared to 15 per cent still in private hands.[12]

This important measure was followed by many other important ones, but as the months went by after the guerrilla's military victory, it became clear that Castro was in no hurry to call elections. Using the argument that the situation was not stable enough to permit the organization of polls, he instead created armed militias to help defend the Revolution, and continued to rule by decree. Although the 26th of July Movement enjoyed considerable support, there was no mass political organization which could form the basis for the exercise of power by the new regime – apart from the communists in the PSP. Until Fidel and his fellow revolutionaries could build up a political base, it was the *barbudos* from the revolutionary war who took complete charge. They imposed change from above, without consulting any of the people affected by the new measures. On 21 May 1959 Fidel declared:

> Our revolution is neither capitalist nor communist! . . . Capitalism sacrifices the human being, communism with its totalitarian conceptions sacrifices human rights. We agree neither with the one nor with the other. Our revolution is not red but olive green. It bears the colour of the rebel army from the Sierra Maestra.

Castro's opponents in Miami have often maintained that rather than olive green, his Revolution was always a 'watermelon': nationalist green on the outside, communist red on the inside. Many thousands of pages have been used up trying to establish at exactly what point in his life Castro became a convinced communist. Other writers have tried to show that his adoption of Marxist economic and political thought was a gradual process. In *My Life*, Castro himself says:

> I strongly supported Martí and his thinking. I had read virtually everything there was to read on the wars of independence; I became acquainted with economic concepts and the absurdities of capitalism and developed my own utopian way of thinking – a utopian socialism, rather than scientific socialism.[13]

In the early months of the new regime, he continued to interpret the Revolution to suit the current Cuban situation and his own view of how earlier revolutions had succeeded or failed. In the Second Declaration of Havana on 4 February 1962 he outlined basic Marxist concepts about society and production and the inevitable triumph of its ideas, and yet at the same time felt confident enough to declare that the Cuban Revolution could spread throughout Latin America, whether or not the 'objective' Marxist conditions for revolution were present. Once again, this revolutionary triumph was to be built on guerrilla struggle rather than the gains made by local communist parties. Both he and Che Guevara believed that revolution could be achieved by a small group of committed revolutionaries, and that those same people could then help create a mass political consciousness that would recognize the value of the gains made. This conviction later put him at odds with the regime leaders in Moscow, as well as with communists in many Latin American nations (which was to be one of the factors for the disastrous failure of Che's guerrilla adventure in Bolivia only a few years later).[14]

Castro's ambiguous political rhetoric, as well as the radical measures decreed in the first few months of the Revolution, convinced many thousands of professional, middle-class Cubans – most of whom had welcomed the fall of Batista's corrupt regime – that what was taking its place was not for them. By the end of the first year of the Revolution, the first great exodus of Cubans had headed across the Florida Straits to the United States.

This exodus only served to exacerbate what quickly became the most difficult foreign issue for the new revolutionary regime. Under Batista in the 1950s, U.S. companies ran the utilities on the island, owned most of the sugar plantations (which took up more than 80 per cent of agricultural land) and the other major agricultural exporting concerns. Nearly all capital goods and infrastructure needs were imported from the United States.

Meeting the 'barbudo' in Washington, DC, 1959.

American business interests – often connected to the Mafia – controlled its hotel and gambling businesses, almost exclusively for American tourists. The Eisenhower administration had propped Batista up until almost the very end, and was jittery about any change on the island. Fidel had repeatedly declared that revolutionary Cuba needed to assert its independence from the United States.

However, at first he did not give the impression of being openly hostile to Washington. In April 1959 he went on a tour of the United States, invited by the American Society of Newspaper Editors. Although President Eisenhower made sure he was conveniently otherwise engaged (playing golf), Castro did meet Vice-President Richard Nixon and many other officials. He consistently sought to allay their fears that Cuba was rapidly converting to communism.

Despite this, over the next few years any chance of mutual tolerance and respect in the bilateral relationship was lost as the United States stepped up its pressure and Castro responded, as he always did when challenged, by resisting and trying to turn the threat to his own advantage. From the early 1960s onwards, the aggressive attitude of Cuba's largest and most important neighbour allowed the Cuban leader not only to justify clamping down on individual rights in the face of an external threat, but to help Cubans accept that his government could not keep all its promises because of the effort needed to counteract the threat from 'American imperialism'.

By 1960 Cuba was already being drawn, willingly or not, into the global Cold War. On the Soviet side, in February 1960 Soviet Deputy Prime Minister Anastas Mikoyan visited Cuba. He offered the new Cuban regime a trade credit of u.s. $100 million, and signed an agreement to buy sugar in exchange for oil. In May 1960 diplomatic relations with the USSR were re-established, eight years after Batista had severed them. When the oil refineries run by American and other foreign companies such as Texaco, Shell and Esso refused to process the first Soviet oil that arrived thanks to this deal, the Cuban authorities confiscated them. This marked the start of a rapid deterioration in relations with the United States. In July 1960 President Eisenhower suspended the u.s. purchase of Cuban sugar, the most important source of foreign revenue for the island. In response, on 6 August 1960 the Cuban

Ernest Hemingway, seen here with Castro in 1960, was wary of the Castro Revolution.

authorities nationalized all u.s.-owned oil and sugar refineries, plus the electricity and phone companies. In September 1960, Castro took the argument to the UN General Assembly in New York, where in his fiercest anti-imperialist mode he declared: 'do away with the philosophy of plunder and you will have done away forever with the philosophy of war!' His tirade lasted almost four-and-a-half hours, and remains the longest-ever speech to the UN General Assembly.

On his return to Cuba, the process of nationalization was stepped up. Law 890 was promulgated, nationalizing 376 foreign-owned enterprises. Their owners were ousted without compensation. At the same time, over three million acres of u.s.-owned land was taken into state hands, as well as some two million acres that had Cuban owners. Once again, the Eisenhower administration retaliated in kind. The end of October 1960 saw the ban on u.s. exports to Cuba of all goods apart from food and medicine – a ban which has been in force ever since. In December of the same year, the United States cut its imports of sugar from the island to zero.

In less than two years since coming to power, whether deliberately or not Castro had succeeded in freeing the island from its reliance on the 'colossus of the north'. At the same time, however, he had created the conditions for an open conflict that would have the gravest consequences for Cuba and the entire world.

4

Missiles and Marxism

The year 1961 saw the rift between the Castro regime and Washington turn to violent confrontation. On 3 January 1961 the United States broke off diplomatic relations with Cuba and closed its embassy in Havana. Since 1959, the Eisenhower administration had been financing and training anti-Castro Cubans with the aim of toppling his regime. When the young and inexperienced John F. Kennedy won the presidency in 1960, he inherited plans for a land invasion of Cuban exiles on the island, to be backed up by air strikes and possible armed support from u.s. troops.

On 17 April 1961, as many as 1,500 counter-revolutionaries in the so-called 'Brigade 2506' landed at Playa Girón and Playa Larga, in the Bay of Pigs in the southwest of the island. As commander-in-chief of the revolutionary armed forces, Fidel Castro assumed direct command of the defences, at the head of a citizens' militia some 250,000 strong. President Kennedy refused to commit u.s. combat troops or planes to the invasion attempt, leaving the Cubans isolated. The exiles had also been counting on popular uprisings on the island to help them oust the revolutionary government, but these never materialized. As a result, the invaders were defeated in less than three days, with more than 100 killed, although losses among the defending forces were considerably higher. Some 1,300 members of the invading force were taken prisoner: of these, fourteen were put on trial for abuses they were alleged to have committed under the Batista regime, and five were executed.

But the most striking aspect of the way the others were treated was that Castro once again turned the occasion into a media event – with himself in the starring role. On live television in Cuba he personally discussed their reasons for wanting to attack the island with a large group of the would-be invaders. He also sent ten of the prisoners back to the United States to help conduct negotiations for the release of the whole group, trusting their word of honour that they would return to Cuba – which they did.[1] In December 1962 the remaining prisoners were finally exchanged for u.s. $53 million in medicine and foodstuffs and sent back to the United States.

The defeat of the cia-backed exiles strengthened Castro's hand at home and abroad. The victory cemented his position as the head of the armed forces, thus undermining any challenge to his authority from that quarter. The threat from outside also unified the Cuban people behind him, and won him support throughout Latin America and the rest of the Third World, where many countries were struggling to achieve independence from the colonial powers that had previously dominated them. The invasion attempt also pushed Fidel to a closer definition of what kind of society he saw the Revolution creating. On May Day 1961 he openly declared to the crowd in Revolution Square in Havana that the Cuban Revolution was socialist:

> We must talk of a new constitution . . . a constitution contributing to a new social system without the exploitation of man by man. That new social system is called socialism . . . education, the dignity of man, civil rights for women, secure old age, artistic freedom, nationalization of monopolies, and the necessities of life . . . is the program of our socialist revolution.

More than twenty years later, Castro gave his biographer Tad Szulc his assessment of the effect of the United States's early hostility to the Revolution in Cuba:

We were carrying out our programme little by little. All these aggressions accelerated the revolutionary process. Were they the cause? No, this would be an error . . . In Cuba we were going to construct socialism in the most orderly possible manner, within a reasonable period of time, with the least amount of trauma and problems, but the aggressions of imperialism accelerated the revolutionary process.[2]

Castro used the optimism and enthusiasm that followed the defeat of the u.s.-sponsored invaders to press on with more social reforms. Partly because many members of Brigade 2506 had claimed to be devout Catholics, all private schools (including the Jesuit-run colleges where he and his brother had studied) were brought under state control in 1961, and attacks on the Catholic Church as another colonial vestige were stepped up. At the same time, thousands of volunteers were enrolled for a vast Cuban Literacy Campaign, aimed at teaching an estimated one million Cubans to read and write. The political advantages of this effort were obvious, but it was also the kind of social experiment promoted by Che Guevara so that *brigadistas* from the towns and cities would learn something of the realities of life in the Cuban countryside, with the aim of promoting not just literacy but revolutionary solidarity.

Castro also took the opportunity to bring the various competing political groups in Cuba more directly under his control. In July 1961, the 26th of July Movement, the University of Havana Students Revolutionary Directorate, and the People's Socialist Party (Communist Party of Cuba) became unified as the Integrated Revolutionary Organizations (ORI). Following a tussle with the hard-line Communists, who still saw themselves as the organization which should spearhead revolutionary change, in 1963 the ORI became the United Party of the Socialist Revolution (PURS), which in turn in 1965 became the Communist Party of Cuba (PCC) – the Castro Communist Party, as one opposition figure dubbed it.

After the Bay of Pigs fiasco, the Kennedy administration looked for other ways to turn the screws on the Castro regime. At the insistence of the United States, Cuba was expelled from the Organization of American States, the most important forum for debate between all the countries of the western hemisphere (in 1964, Cuba also withdrew from the IMF). This was followed in February 1962 by the announcement of a complete economic and trade embargo of the island, with a ban on all imports. As a direct consequence of this move, March 1962 saw the start of rationing in Cuba, which has persisted in one form or other ever since.

For his part, the Soviet leader Nikolai Khrushchev was keen to test out the new leader in the White House. According to Nikolai Leonov, the KGB's top adviser on Latin American affairs in the 1960s:

> He very much wanted to put a hedgehog down the trousers of the United States. He was very much upset that the USSR was surrounded by American military bases in places like Turkey and Italy. After the Bay of Pigs there was a second very important reason, and that was the defence of the Cuban revolution. So there were the two factors that made Khrushchev want to deploy missiles in Cuba.[3]

Early in 1962, Cuba and the Soviet Union had concluded a secret defence treaty which involved basing more than 40,000 Soviet troops on the island, dispatching a Soviet fleet to Cuban waters, and most controversially, installing medium and long-range missiles capable of carrying nuclear warheads. Castro hoped that this treaty would mean that any further threat of invasion by the United States or Cuban exiles would draw the Soviet Union into the defence of Cuba.

There has been much debate among historians as to why Khrushchev was willing to take such a dangerous step, which took

Meeting Nikita Krushchev at the United Nations in New York in the early 1960s.

the Cold War out of its European theatre and seemed to pose a direct threat to the territory of the United States. One explanation offered is that he was genuinely alarmed at the u.s. installation of Jupiter missiles in Turkey and Italy, which posed a direct threat to the Soviet Union and its Eastern European allies. Khrushchev also doubtless sensed that the Bay of Pigs rout had shown the young, inexperienced Kennedy to be hesitant about using force, and that if he pressured him over Cuba, he might be able to gain an advantage in what to him was a more important area: control over Berlin.

For his part, Kennedy had been stung by the failed invasion attempt, and by attacks from the Republicans that he was a weak president who was allowing communism to gain ground in Europe, Asia, and now the u.s. backyard of the Caribbean. From the moment of his inauguration in 1960, he had stated that one of his main foreign affairs priorities was to get rid of Castro and his regime. After the Bay of Pigs, he authorized Operation Mongoose, designed to support counter-revolutionary groups in Cuba, as well as direct attempts by the CIA to eliminate Castro. Recently published tape-recordings suggest that the Pentagon was actively making plans for an invasion of the island, with or without the participation of Cuban exiles.

Then on 14 October 1962 came the bombshell. U.S. spy planes provided the Kennedy administration with photographic evidence that the Soviets had built missile sites on the island – although there did not as yet appear to be any missiles installed with nuclear warheads. Over the next fifteen days, the world came as close as it ever had to a nuclear war between the two superpowers. Kennedy saw this as a confrontation with the Soviet Union, with Cuba as a pretext. The main choices facing him and his advisers were whether to launch air strikes to destroy the missile installations, or air strikes followed by an all-out invasion. This was the option favoured by the military chiefs of staff. The president however, who was wary of the Pentagon and the CIA after what he saw as poor advice over the Bay of Pigs fiasco, supported by his brother Bobby and Secretary of Defense Robert McNamara, argued for a third option: a blockade against the Soviet ships bringing in the missile warheads, plus negotiations with Khrushchev to find a diplomatic way out of the conflict. Those who argued for this more nuanced response even brought in a comparison with Pearl Harbor: what would become of the United States's supposed moral authority in the world if it employed similar tactics to the Japanese, who had struck without warning against the U.S. fleet in 1941? Over the next few days, this more cautious approach gradually gained ground, although the Soviet ships continued their advance towards the Caribbean. The whole world held its breath as the countdown to nuclear war appeared to have begun.

At almost the last moment, on 27 October 1962, the Soviets backed down. Their ships turned round, and U.S. personnel were

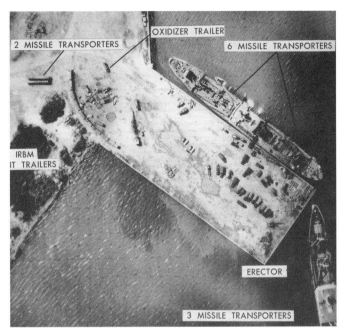

Soviet missile sites in Cuba photographed by a U.S. spy plane.

even allowed to board one of them to inspect the cargo. This climb-down came as a result of frantic efforts to find a diplomatic solution that would allow both sides to save face. Khrushchev sent two letters to Kennedy, one for public consumption, one in private. In the latter, he agreed to withdraw the missiles and dismantle the bases, if Kennedy secretly agreed to withdraw the U.S. missiles from Italy and Turkey, and to give a formal statement that the United States would not invade Cuba in order to topple the Castro regime.

Fidel Castro was furious that all the negotiation and bargaining went on without him even being consulted. He was taught a sharp lesson: that he may be an ally of the Soviet Union, but that the real struggle was between the two superpowers. Cuba was nothing more than a pawn in that game. Looking back on these dramatic events more than 40 years later, his sense of wounded pride is still evident:

> We learned from news reports that the Soviets were making the proposal to withdraw the missiles. And it had never been discussed with us in any way! We weren't opposed to a solution, because it was important to avoid a nuclear conflict. But Khrushchev should have told the Americans, 'The Cubans must be included in the discussions.' At that moment they lost their nerve, and they weren't firm in their determination. Out of principle, they should have consulted with us.[4]

In recent years, it has come to light that both Castro and Che Guevara urged Khrushchev not only to refuse to back down, but also to launch a pre-emptive nuclear strike on u.s. cities. Some historians have even suggested that this gung-ho attitude from Fidel and his revolutionary companions may even have contributed to the Soviet leader's decision to back off.

Despite Castro's anger, the missile crisis resulted in several positive results for Cuba. The presence of increased numbers of Soviet military personnel acted as a guarantee against any further aggressive move by the United States, and President Kennedy's promise not to invade seems to have been genuine. He reined in the Pentagon and its invasion plans, but could also claim to his critics that he had stood up to the Soviet bully. Fidel Castro, however, was the one who as usual claimed the moral high ground, declaring on 1 November 1962: 'We possess moral long-range missiles that cannot be dismantled and will never be dismantled. This is our strongest strategic weapon.'[5] At the same time, Castro seems to have had considerable respect for his u.s. counterpart. President Kennedy emerged from the missile crisis with greater confidence in his own abilities. In 1963 he brought in the progressive Human

Rights Act, and the overthrow of Castro ceased to be a foreign policy priority. Indeed, there are suggestions that he was willing to seek an accommodation with the Cuban leader, who was also apparently open to at least the idea of talking with the United States. The first tentative messages were exchanged in October 1963, only to come to nothing with Kennedy's assassination in Dallas on 22 November.[6] One of the wilder conspiracy theories surrounding the president's murder is that it was a plot by Miami Cubans worried that the two leaders could in fact reach some sort of compromise. According to Halperin, it was only when U.S. troops sent in by President Johnson invaded the Dominican Republic in April 1965 that Fidel Castro finally gave up on the idea of rapprochement with the United States.

After the deal between the Soviet Union and the United States had been done, Soviet Foreign Minister Anastas Mikoyan was again despatched to Havana to smooth things over. He left after three weeks, having had little success. Khrushchev himself was more successful, with the result that in May 1963 Fidel went on his first trip to the Soviet Union on a visit that lasted more than a month. He was received as an honoured guest, appearing on the podium at the May Day parade and being feted at dinners and ceremonies. At the same time, on his tour of many different regions in the Soviet Union he was able to see at first hand – and for the first time – how the centralised socialist economic system actually functioned. This visit led him to come down on the side of the Soviets in their dispute with the Chinese, and also to shy away from attempts at diversification and industrialization back in Cuba as advocated by Che Guevara, who by now was Minister of Industries.

During a second visit to Moscow in January 1964, Castro signed a long-term deal for the Soviet Union to purchase the bulk of Cuba's sugar harvest at a higher price than the international rate, while Cuba imported industrial machinery and even entire factories from the Soviet Union. Cuba was committed to export five million tons of sugar that year, while according to the five-year plan for 1965–70 (elaborated in conjunction with Soviet experts), this was set to rise to ten million tons in 1970, as revolutionary productivity worked its wonders. Castro's view was that sugar exports, particularly thanks to beneficial deals with the socialist bloc, could bring in sufficient foreign currency to enable Cuba to buy industrial and other equipment. This would then help kick-start indigenous industry and lead within a few years to a significant broadening of the Cuban economy. His calculation proved to be wildly over-optimistic, and has been one of the major weaknesses in his regime's economic management ever since. In addition to its payments for sugar, by the mid-1960s the Soviet Union was delivering aid to the tune of u.s. $1 million per day into Cuba,[7] and as ever, that aid came with political strings attached.

Although Fidel took Cuba decisively into the Soviet zone of influence, in the mid-1960s he was also stepping up support for revolutionary efforts within Latin America, even though local Communist Party tactics were often at odds with these guerrilla initiatives. As Castro had declared in the Second Declaration of Havana on 4 February 1962, 'the duty of every revolutionary is to make the revolution'. He followed this up by offering assistance to left-wing groups in Peru, Venezuela, Colombia, and of course in 1967 to Che Guevara's ill-fated foray into the bleak highlands of eastern Bolivia. Beyond the American continent, Castro was also keen to show his support for the newly independent countries of Africa and Asia. In October 1963, at the request of Algerian president Ahmed Ben Bella, Castro sent tanks and troops to Algeria to help repel an invasion by neighbouring Morocco. This was the start of active Cuban involvement in Africa that was to last for more than twenty years. Castro was keen to prove that revolutionary solidarity was something more than just a fine phrase, while Khrushchev and subsequent leaders in Moscow found it useful to have a proxy power supporting the 'socialist' ideal throughout the developing world.

Relations with the United States remained frozen, while it became the destination of choice for Cubans unwilling to accept the new regime. In the first three years after the Revolution, an estimated 200,000 people left the island, including some 14,000 children who were sent off for adoption in what was known as *Operación Pedro Pan*. In 1965, in the so-called 'Camarioca incident', almost 3,000 Cubans were allowed to leave by boat for Florida, setting the precedent for several mass exoduses which showed the frustration felt by many ordinary Cubans at the increase in state control over their lives, as well as the continuous call for greater efforts and austerity in their daily existence. Within his own family, Fidel's sister Emma left for Mexico in the early 1960s, while his divorced wife Mirta Díaz-Balart had lived in Miami since the mid-1950s. Fidel's younger sister Juanita joined her in 1964, in what was fast becoming Cuba's capital city in exile.

Once the u.s. trade embargo had been put in place, it was more difficult for Cubans to get exit visas, but, as Richard Gott details in *Cuba: A New History*, 'freedom flights began in 1965'.[8] Over the next six years, until they were scrapped by incoming President Richard Nixon, '3,000 flights had brought more than a quarter of a million Cubans (260,561) into exile in the United States'. Many of those who left were the liberal professional classes or business people, especially after 1968, when the last private businesses were expropriated. Castro ordered the closure of all private enterprises, declaring that there was no place in the new Cuba for that 'small segment of the population that lives off the work of others, living considerably better than the rest, sitting idly by and looking on while others do the work'. This drain of human resources was keenly felt in the new Cuban society being created, as in many areas there were few skilled people left to help plan the growth and modernization that Castro hoped for. Not that the regime ever

With Raúl and
Che Guevara in
1963.

recognized the values of any of these exiles: they were soon dubbed
as *gusanos*, worms who had turned against the Revolution.

When Batista and his family fled into exile at the very end of
1958, it was Che Guevara who, together with Camilo Cienfuegos,
led the triumphant guerrilla forces into Havana. These two men,
and to a lesser extent Fidel's brother Raúl, were seen by most
Cubans as the heroes of the Revolution. Che began to record
their shared experiences in the guerrilla war, writing what were
to become the classic books on guerrilla fighting, *Guerrilla Warfare*
and *Reminiscences of the Cuban Revolutionary War*. This set the
pattern for him to be the reflective half of the partnership, while
Fidel was immersed in the day-to-day struggle of creating and
running the new government.

It was no easy task to establish a government that could ensure
that the euphoria of the overthrow of the dictatorship was harnessed
and put to use to fundamentally change Cuban society once and
for all. However, Che and Fidel's other most trusted associates
became closely involved in drawing up new legislation such as the
agrarian reform law, the legislation on property and basic individual rights. To do this, Raúl, Fidel's old associate Alfredo Guevara,
and the rest of the inner circle met in the villa in Tarará outside
Havana into which Che had now moved. Fidel would join them to

discuss their draft legislation late in the night. His opinion almost invariably held sway, although there was a great deal of improvisation and many last-minute changes. Alfredo Guevara, for example, never tires of regaling people with the story of how Che became the governor of the Central Bank. According to Alfredo, Fidel came to the villa in the early hours one morning, and asked which of them was a good economist. To the surprise of all those present, Che said enthusiastically that he was. 'Good,' said Fidel, 'then you can take over the Central Bank because the director Felipe Pazos has just resigned'. When Alfredo asked Che what he knew about economics, Che turned pale and said: 'Economics? I thought he asked 'who's a good communist?'⁹

By this time, Che had officially become Cuban. One of the earliest moves Fidel made after the revolutionary victory was to include in the new constitution the provision that anyone with the rank of '*comandante*' in the guerrilla army who had served for more than a year should be given full Cuban citizenship – and the only person to whom this applied was the Argentine revolutionary.¹⁰

The early years of the Revolution saw a great amount of debate as to what exactly socialism might mean in a country such as Cuba, with an economy based on agriculture and with little heavy industry. Fidel enlisted Che's support to thwart the attempts of Aníbal Escalante and the Partido Socialista Popular (the Communist Party of Cuba) to take over the running of the government, replacing it with a Communist party that was loyal to him first and only afterwards to Moscow. But the two men soon diverged on the question not only of their own allegiance to the Soviets, but also on what constituted the most appropriate approach to a planned socialist economy in Cuba. To Che, Nikita Khrushchev's climbdown over the missile crisis in October 1962 was a further sign that Soviet communism had betrayed its revolutionary principles. He was far more impressed with the brand of socialism Mao Tse-Tung was trying to create in China, considering that like Cuba, the revolution there had emerged out of a peasant guerrilla war. As Minister for Industries in the early 1960s, Che was also convinced that Cuba should not simply buy machinery and capital goods from the Soviet bloc, but should attempt to move away from its dependence on agricultural exports – still predominantly sugar – and try to industrialize. Here perhaps his experience of Argentina in the 1940s and early 1950s had persuaded him that the way out of dependency was by strengthening national industry. He also insisted in texts such as *Man and Socialism in Cuba* that in order for the revolution to prosper politically and economically, it needed to insist on sacrifice and the collective good. By proving that the Revolution was morally superior to capitalism, he argued, it could take the mass of the population with it. 'Socialist emulation' would replace exploitation by bosses or indeed by the state.

Fidel however was not convinced. By the mid-1960s he had signed co-operation deals with the Soviet Union and its allies that reinforced Cuba's dependence on them, as well as substituting the Soviet Union for the United States as the buyer of the island's sugar crop at advantageous prices. Within a few years, the Castro regime had exchanged Cuba's dependency on the United States for an equally unbalanced relationship with the Soviet Union and its Eastern European allies. And despite the fact that he was keenly aware that the continuing success of the regime depended on the development of a revolutionary awareness among everyone, Fidel was more concerned with laying the institutional basis for this in education and the workplace.

In addition to their different views on the direction revolutionary Cuba should take in economic policy, Fidel and Che did not see eye to eye on the possibility of fomenting revolution in other countries. Fidel seems in these early years to have at least partially accepted the Moscow line that revolutionary change could most successfully be brought about through the development of local Communist parties and the creation of working-class consciousness that would

With Che Guevara in the mid-1960s.

eventually lead to the overthrow of repressive regimes in Latin America and elsewhere. Che saw the guerrilla success in Cuba as being a model for other countries throughout the world. He also supported Mao's view that a revolution must be permanent if it is to avoid congealing into privilege with the emergence of a new bureaucratic class that has not been through the dangers and rigours of the combat that led to the victory of the Revolution in the first place.

The greatest difference between the two men was that whereas Fidel had largely fulfilled his dream of liberating his native country, for Che the revolutionary struggle in Cuba was only the beginning. His belief in the possibility of exporting the 'Cuban model' of guerrilla warfare, with a small group or *foco* of determined fighters spearheading the struggle against repressive regimes from rural strongholds far from the centres of power is what took Che, with Fidel's blessing, to the Congo in 1965. However, the attempt to copy the experience of the Sierra Maestra in the mountains of the eastern Congo quickly proved to be a disaster. By October 1965, Che was writing: 'We cannot liberate a country that does not want to fight'. From the diaries he edited after his withdrawal from the country, it is clear that Che had little knowledge of the beliefs or practices of the Africans whom he was meant to be liberating: in Cuba he at least shared a language with the oppressed peasants, and centuries of a comparable tradition. In the Congo he and the rest of the Cubans had only theoretical knowledge of the kind of war they wanted to fight, and failed miserably. Worse still, at that very moment Fidel Castro chose to make public in Cuba the private letter Che had written him shortly before his departure in March of that year. In it, Che renounced his Cuban citizenship and said farewell to all official positions in the revolutionary government. Fidel claimed he was revealing the contents of the letter at that time because he was busy appointing a new central committee of the Cuban Communist party, and there would have been speculation as to why Guevara was not included. Critics and opponents of Fidel Castro have been harsher, arguing that Fidel saw the chance to cut Che adrift and rid himself of a possible rival for power, and took advantage of the situation with his usual alacrity. Whatever the truth of the matter, there is no doubt that Che felt he had been betrayed by Fidel, as the publication of the letter completely undermined his position not only as the leader of the Cubans in the Congo, but also with the rebel groups they were meant to be supporting.

The humiliating retreat followed shortly afterwards. As Che licked his wounds in Dar es Salaam, and wrote his customary account of what he had no compunction about calling 'a failure', it was plain he had no intention of returning to Cuba. Fidel Castro has put this down to the Argentine's sense of hurt pride,[11] and yet it is clear that the sense of being abandoned went far deeper than that. After Dar es Salaam, Che was moved to a safe house in Prague, while Fidel had to decide what to do with him. He himself was busy backing the guerrilla movements in several South American countries, and also attacked the idea of 'peaceful co-existence' which was the then current Moscow line on relations with the West.

Knowing that Che was determined to continue the struggle within Latin America, Fidel spent several months discussing where the most promising target might be. Che was known to want to eventually bring the Revolution to his own country of Argentina, but recent guerrilla attempts there had been crushed. He was also keen to go to Peru, where his first wife Hilda Gadea had long been active in revolutionary efforts. Eventually however, it seems as if the two men settled on Bolivia. This landlocked country in the heart of Latin America was not only one of the poorest on the continent, but had recently been taken over by a repressive military regime. Fidel, mindful of what had happened when the guerrillas had first begun their struggle in Cuba, tried opening talks with leaders of the strong Bolivian Communist party, in order to build some kind of political front. He has said that he also tried to persuade Guevara to wait for conditions to be more favourable, but that his old companion-in-arms was too 'impatient'.

In November 1965, disguised as a balding Uruguayan businessman (he and Fidel apparently took great pleasure in the fact that not even Raúl recognized him) Guevara arrived in La Paz, the capital of Bolivia. He soon left for the country's eastern jungle region, with fewer than 40 followers. Despite this, according to Jon Lee Anderson, author of the most complete biography on Che Guevara, his revolutionary plans were already nothing if not ambitious:

> From his crude camp in the Bolivian outback, Che foresaw an astonishing, even fantastic sequence of events – and starting the war and spreading it to the neighbouring nations were only the first two stages. In the third stage, wars in South America would

draw in the Americans. This intervention would benefit the guerrillas by giving their campaigns a nationalistic hue; as in Vietnam, they would be fighting against a foreign invader. And by deploying forces in Latin America, the United States would be more dispersed and, ultimately, weaker on all fronts, in Bolivia as well as in Vietnam. Finally, the spreading conflagration would lead China and Russia to stop their feuding and align forces with the revolutionaries everywhere to bring down u.s. imperialism once and for all.[12]

In the second week of October 1967, Che was captured and then executed in the tiny village of La Higuera. Fidel at first could not believe the reports, but when he was convinced, he immediately named 8 October as the 'Day of the Heroic Guerrilla' in Che's honour. Ten days later he addressed a crowd of close to a million in Plaza de la Revolución in Havana. He concluded his passionate eulogy with words that also show his awareness that building a revolutionary society in Cuba required still further efforts:

> If we want the . . . model of a human being who does not belong to our time but to the future, I say from the depths of my heart that such a model, without a single stain on his conduct, without a single stain on his behaviour, is Che! If we wish to express what we want our children to be, we must say from our very hearts as ardent revolutionaries: we want them to be like Che![13]

This was not quite the end of the story. Castro also named the year 1968 in Che's honour, and often held him up as a moral example to young revolutionaries. A coda to their friendship took place 30 years later in 1997. After he had been shot, Che's body (minus the hands, which had been cut off, allegedly for identification purposes) had been buried under the airstrip of the small town of Vallegrande in the southeast of the country. In July 1997, with a democratic government installed in La Paz, a Cuban-Argentine forensic team, using techniques learned from identifying the bodies of those 'disappeared' during the military dictatorship in Argentina, found and identified Guevara's remains. In October they were flown back to Cuba, where they were received by Fidel and Raúl. Later that month they were placed in a vast mausoleum built on the outskirts of Santa Clara, where Che had helped the guerrilla forces win a decisive battle almost 40 years earlier. Once again, Fidel Castro praised his former colleague, this time stressing his moral qualities in a directly biblical fashion:

> Why did they think that by killing him, he would cease to exist as a fighter? Today he is in every place, wherever there is a just cause to defend. His indelible mark is now in history and his luminous gaze of a prophet has become a symbol for all the poor of this world.

The other possible challenge to Fidel Castro's ascendancy in the early months of the Revolution came from Camilo Cienfuegos (Fidel's brother Raúl appears to have always accepted his own subordinate role). Cienfuegos had been a charismatic fighter in the mountains, and was appointed chief of the general staff in the revolutionary army. Whereas Guevara saw himself as a theorist, Camilo was the romantic rebel hero, dressed as a Cuban peasant and closest to the common man in the countryside. He does not seem to have had personal ambitions to hold more power after the guerrilla victory, and remained one of Fidel's most trusted lieutenants. It was to him that Castro turned when he had to deal with one of the most serious threats to the new regime: the resignation of Huber Matos, one of Castro's associates since the days of the Ortodoxo party in the early 1950s. After the rebel victory, Matos had been appointed military commander of the sensitive region of Camagüey, where cattle ranchers had opposed the new agrarian reform law and the Catholic Church was concerned about plans to change the educational system. However, when Raúl Castro was appointed head of the revolutionary armed forces in October 1959, Matos wrote an open letter to Fidel offering his resignation, saying that this was due to what he saw as an increasing communist influence within the government. Suspecting a plot against him, Castro rushed to Camagüey, where he had Matos and a score of his military subordinates arrested. Castro replaced Matos with Camilo Cienfuegos, whom he knew he could trust. Cienfuegos died soon afterwards when the small plane he was travelling in back to Havana disappeared, never to be found. In exile circles, it was maintained for many years that this was no accident, and that Fidel himself had ordered Cienfuegos' death as he also suspected his loyalty. No proof for this theory has ever been given.

In one of the last show trials of the early days of the Revolution, Huber Matos was found guilty of 'betraying the revolution'. Raúl Castro apparently pressed for the death sentence, but in the end Matos was given twenty years in jail on the Isla de Pinos, where Castro had been incarcerated a few years earlier. Matos served the full term, for many years in solitary confinement, and now lives in Miami, where he is still active in opposition to Castro.

Although the Cuban exiles in the Bay of Pigs incursion did not receive support from anti-Castro elements on the island, there was considerable unrest during the early years of the revolutionary government. It was in the southern Escambray mountains that the most serious threat emerged. At one point in the early 1960s there were said to be some 3,000 men fighting against the new regime. Fidel was always insistent that these insurgents – a mixture of small landowners, rural workers, disaffected former Castro supporters – were nothing more than 'bandits'. It is true that they lacked any coherent ideology apart from their opposition to his regime; they also lacked real leaders and a true sense of purpose. Nevertheless, as Tad Szulc says:

these were costly operations, and Castro's casualties reached over three hundred killed in Escambray alone; economic losses were calculated at around U.S. $1 billion in ruined crops, burned houses, destroyed rolling stock, roads and bridges – not to mention the military coast of the 'anti-bandit' operations.[14]

The last of the Escambray fighters were not rounded up until 1966.

In addition to these challenges to the regime he was busy putting in place, Fidel Castro was himself the direct target of multiple assassination attempts. A former head of the Cuban Intelligence Services, Fabián Escalante, has detailed in a recently published book the '638 ways to kill Fidel Castro' that he claimed personally to be aware of. Within days of Fidel Castro's triumph over the Batista forces, the CIA was plotting ways to get rid of the new leader. By October 1959, the U.S. president Dwight D. Eisenhower had approved a CIA proposal to take covert action against Castro's government, with the aim 'to topple Castro in one year and replace him with a junta friendly to the United States'. There was also White House support for clandestine radio operations to bolster pro-U.S. opposition groups within Cuba, in the hope that these counter-revolutionaries could establish a controlled area on the island which could be declared a 'free' Cuba, and authorization for attempts to eliminate Castro himself.

After the Bay of Pigs catastrophe, President Kennedy continued to give money and support to clandestine efforts to get rid of Castro personally and to overthrow his regime. In March 1962, Operation Mongoose was launched, under the direct control of Bobby Kennedy as Attorney General. The plan was to develop ways of sabotaging and undermining the Castro regime by stealth. Although Operation Mongoose was officially closed after the Cuban Missile Crisis in October 1962 as a result of President Kennedy's promise not to attempt to invade Cuba, the CIA and other agencies continued to train and support Cuban exiles. This meant that by the mid-1960s the CIA station in Miami was the largest outside its headquarters in Langley, Virginia. As Ann Louise Bardach puts it:

> Its staff feverishly threw itself into planning all kinds of inventive, often hilarious, schemes to remove Fidel Castro. There would be exploding cigars, beard defoliants intended to emasculate the Cuban leader, and a succession of Mata Hari sirens trained to transmit the kiss of death.[15]

The then Interior Minister of Cuba, Ramiro Valdés, has said that in 1964–5 there were as many as 30 attempts on the Cuban leader's life, including one involving a cyanide capsule in a milkshake that very nearly succeeded.[16] Perhaps the most outlandish of these plots is quoted in Sebastian Balfour's *Castro: Profiles in Power*. This apparently came out of a suggestion at a dinner party with the Kennedys by Ian Fleming, the creator of James Bond. The plan was

> to spread rumours around the island that the Saviour was about to return to Earth to denounce Castro as an anti-Christ; on the appointed day, a bearded CIA frogman would emerge on a beach in Cuba claiming to be Christ while an American submarine would surface just over the horizon shooting star shells into the sky.[17]

As the end of the first decade of revolutionary rule approached, Fidel Castro was the undisputed leader of the government and the Communist Party of Cuba. The next few years saw little of the high drama of the early 1960s. Instead, for good or ill, Castro oversaw the creation of more permanent institutions on the island, and closer integration with the Soviet bloc. He himself looked beyond his home country and sought to play an important role on the international stage.

5

Revolution and the State

The year 1968 saw mass protests on the streets from Paris to Chicago, London to Mexico. Young people in particular demonstrated against imperialism and proposed a new, less rigid kind of socialism that could offer more inspiration than the stale formulas offered by out-of-touch leaders such as General de Gaulle or Lyndon B. Johnson. In the Soviet sphere of influence, the 'Prague Spring' saw reformers in the Czech Republic seeking to loosen ties with Moscow and to experiment with their own style of socialism. Many of the youthful protesters saw the revolutionary regime led by Fidel Castro as offering a similarly fresh, more open kind of socialist society that they could look up to and respect. However, for many on the left, this was also the time when that dream proved to be an illusion. After the Soviet invasion of Czechoslovakia in August 1968 and the removal of the reformist Dubček government, Castro took the side of Moscow. Declaring that the situation in Czechoslovakia was 'deteriorating and going downhill on its way back to capitalism', he bizarrely described the Warsaw Pact intervention as preventing the country from 'falling into the arms of imperialism'. Almost 40 years later, in the interviews he gave to the journalist Ignacio Ramonet, collected in *My Life*, he repeated almost exactly the same criticisms of the Czech reformers and repeated that the invasion had been a 'bitter necessity'.[1]

Another great disappointment awaited those international sympathizers on the Left who hoped that the Cuban Revolution would usher in a flowering of creative expression. From the very start, within Cuba there had been clashes over what role culture should play in a revolutionary society. These came to a head as early as 1961, when the newly created ICAIC (Cuban Institute of Cinematographic Art and Industry) refused to show a short documentary, *PM* (produced by the young writers and film-makers associated with the review *Lunes de Revolución*), because it was deemed to be 'counter-revolutionary'. This led to fierce public debates between intellectuals and members of the government, including Che Guevara and Castro. Fidel was already reflecting on how the small 'avant-garde' of revolutionary fighters could win over the vast majority of Cubans who had not taken part in the fight against Batista. He recognized the importance of winning the battle of ideas as well. It was at this point that he made what was to become his second most famous pronouncement, after the 'History will absolve me!' speech in 1953. It is important to quote the passage at length, in order not to distort the meaning, as has so often happened:

The Revolution must try to win the major part of the people over to its ideas. The Revolution must never renounce having the majority of the people with it, having not just the revolutionaries, but also all the honest citizens who are with it even though they are not revolutionaries – that is, even though they do not have a revolutionary attitude toward life. The Revolution should reject only those who are incorrigible reactionaries, who are incorrigible counterrevolutionaries. And the Revolution must have a policy for that part of the people. The Revolution must have an attitude for that part of the intellectuals and writers. The Revolution must understand that reality, and consequently must act in such a way that the entire sector of artists and intellectuals who are not genuinely revolutionary find a place to work and to create within the Revolution, and so that their creative spirit will have an opportunity and freedom for expression within the Revolution, even though they are not revolutionary writers or artists. This means that within the Revolution, everything goes; against the Revolution, nothing.[2]

This declaration was part of widespread debate in the early 1960s as to the role of the intellectual in the emerging revolutionary society. Magazines such as *Cuba Socialista* or *Pensamiento Crítico* discussed what it might take to create what Che Guevara was to call the 'new man'. There was also much discussion of how the Cuban example was different from the 'socialist' societies of the Soviet Union and Eastern Europe, and how the transition to 'true' socialism was to be achieved on the island. But writers who argued in favour of a liberal democratic pluralism of thought, such as those expounded in the magazine *Lunes de Revolución,* soon found that their views were frozen out. Then, as Cuba became increasingly enmeshed with the Soviet Union, so the manuals of 'scientific socialism' became required reading in universities, and textbooks in schools throughout Cuba reflected Marxist thought, without consideration of other traditions. Religious freedom was restricted from 1962, when Cuba was declared an atheist state: most Roman Catholic priests left then or soon afterwards. By the end of the decade, the only daily press functioning was the recently created official newspaper *Granma*. Radio and television were in state hands, and so were the film and book industries. Authors had to belong to the official union, UNEAC (National Union of Writers and Artists of Cuba), if they wanted anything to be published (with the state publishing house). From 1965 onwards there was also a campaign against 'counter-revolutionary' groups and in particular against homosexuals. Many of these were sent to the UMAP (Military Units to Aid Production) forced labour camps, where 'counter-revolutionaries' were made to do harsh agricultural or building work. According to one Cuban-born historian, gays, Catholics, Jehovah's Witnesses, Seventh-Day Adventists, and practitioners of certain Afro-Cuban traditions, such as the secret society of Abakuá, found themselves thrown together doing forced labor as a penalty for deviating from the ruling ideology and practices.[3]

Despite these increasingly restrictive tendencies, in January 1968 the Cuban authorities organized the First Havana Cultural Congress. This drew some 500 writers, artists and thinkers from around the world to discuss the role of culture in a society building a revolution, and showed the participants what the organizers thought had been achieved in the nine years since the Cuban Revolution. An account of the Congress is documented in the Caribbean poet Andrew Salkey's *Havana Journal* of 1971. As had become the custom whenever a large-scale international event took place in Cuba, Fidel Castro closed the congress, speaking of the 'universal conscience of struggle'. However, by the end of that same year, this international support was gravely undermined by what became known as the 'Padilla Affair'. For the Fourth Competition of the National Union of Writers and Artists of Cuba, a jury of international writers awarded the poetry prize to the young poet Heberto Padilla for his collection *Fuera del Juego* (Out of the Game) and the theatre prize to Antón Arrufat. Both of them were critical of the regime. In his poems, Padilla expressed his doubts and concerns about the effect the Revolution was having in Cuba, as well as making jibes at the expense of the Soviet bloc. This led to a huge controversy and constant official attacks on his poetry as 'petty bourgeois' and 'defeatist'.

Padilla was placed under house arrest, and became a marked man. Eventually, in 1971, he was arrested for 'counter-revolutionary activities' and imprisoned. He was only set free after protests from many of the West's leading intellectual figures, including Jean-Paul Sartre (a formerly warm supporter of the Revolution), Susan

Sontag, Octavio Paz and other prominent Latin American writers, but was forced to read a 'self-criticism' statement in public in Havana. The 60 foreign intellectuals who were active in his defence claimed that this treatment recalled 'the most sordid moments of the era of Stalinism, with its prefabricated verdicts and its witch-hunts.' Other important previous supporters of the Revolution, such as the influential French agronomist René Dumont, also warned that Castro refused to allow anyone else to take important political and economic decisions, became sidetracked by grandiose but implausible projects (like the wholesale draining of coastal marshes, establishing a cheese industry in Cuba, for example), while frustration at rationing and being marshalled into government-run mass organizations was growing.[4] Castro responded to these criticisms by rejecting

> the claims of the mafia of pseudo-leftist bourgeois intellectuals to become the critical conscience of society. They are the bearers of a new colonialism, the agents of the metropolitan imperialist culture.[5]

The arguments for and against the Castro regime and its cultural policy were particularly vitriolic among Latin American writers, many of whom were beginning to acquire an international reputation thanks to the so-called 'boom' in fiction from the region, and who were also seen as influential spokesmen on political and social matters. One of Fidel Castro's staunchest friends in this respect has been the Colombian writer Gabriel García Márquez. The Nobel prizewinner has always combined a love of literature with a fascination for politics and the exercise of power. For his part, Fidel Castro has always been drawn to the written word, especially journalism: for many years he was known to read as much foreign press agency material as he could get his hands on every morning. García Márquez's interest in Cuba was first aroused when he learnt of the exploits of Castro and his guerrilla fighters in the Sierra Maestra. In April 1958 he interviewed Fidel's sister Emma Castro in Caracas, where he was then living and working as a journalist. The enthusiastic tone of the interview showed that even then he was a believer in the Revolution and in Castro's ability to lead it.

The opportunity to become more closely involved in building that Revolution came soon after the guerrilla's military victory, when García Márquez was called upon to help set up the *Prensa Latina* news agency. This was designed by Che Guevara and Fidel to act as a counterweight to the 'imperialist' agencies, in order to give a version of the world as seen from the developing countries of the South. It was not long before the difficulties of offering wholehearted support to the Castro regime became obvious to the Colombian author. He attended the public 'Operation Truth' trials of suspected Batista supporters in January 1959, public show trails that more often than not ended in a death sentence summarily carried out. Although Che and Raúl were primarily in charge of the trials, Fidel Castro followed them closely, and it was to him that García Márquez signed a petition calling for one of the condemned men to be reprieved. The appeal for clemency was rejected, and this was later used against García Márquez when he was edged out of *Prensa Latina* by hard-line Communists who were trying to dominate the revolutionary leadership.

Despite being dismissed from *Prensa Latina*, after the Bay of Pigs victory, García Márquez still continued to express his admiration for Castro. Then in 1968 came the aforementioned huge polemic surrounding Heberto Padilla. García Márquez's name appeared on the list that protesting international writers signed in Paris, although he has always insisted it was added without his knowledge. His protests left him in an uncomfortable position: the writers who championed freedom of expression felt they could not count on his support, while the Cuban regime was also aggrieved that he appeared to have joined their 'enemies'. (Padilla was eventually allowed to leave Cuba in 1980, apparently thanks in great measure to the personal intervention of the Colombian writer with Fidel.)

It was not until several years later when García Márquez wrote a long adulatory article about Cuba sending troops to Angola that the two men were reconciled. Since then they have been close friends, taking summer holidays together on the coast or on Castro's motor cruiser *Acuaramas*. On García Márquez's side, the relationship has been based on his fascination with power and the fact that leaders such as Castro have to make decisions affecting the lives of millions, rather than merely entertaining them or moving them with words. In his exhaustive biography of the writer, Gerry Martin concludes: 'Fidel Castro was one of the few things in which he was ever able to believe.'[6]

For his part, the Cuban leader has always been fascinated by the power of words: in his own speeches of course, but also in journalism and on the international stage. García Márquez has also been important in persuading him that despite the rejection of the revolution and the direction it took under his leadership by many liberal intellectuals in the West, he is still able to convince one of the most important writers and intellectuals in Latin America that he is worthy of support.

García Márquez has frequently been taken to task for his continued backing of Castro. Mario Vargas Llosa, who like the Colombian has won the Nobel Prize for Literature, was one of those who distanced himself over the Padilla Affair, and has shown no hesitation in calling him the 'lackey of Fidel Castro'. García Márquez has always maintained that above all he supports Fidel's anti-u.s. imperialist stance, and argues that over the years he has helped many political prisoners win their freedom or for their sentences to be reduced by appealing personally to Castro. The Cuban leader later gave his verdict on their friendship:

We both believe in social justice, in the dignity of man. What characterizes Gabriel is his love of others, his solidarity with others, which is a characteristic of every revolutionary.[7]

On the domestic front, at the end of the 1960s sugar was once more the focus of attention. Ever since the U.S. dominance of the island in the early years of the twentieth century, sugar had dominated agricultural exports and foreign currency earnings. Cuba has ideal growing conditions for the crop, which can produce up to seven years of harvests before the cane needs to be burnt and regenerated. Until the breakdown in relations in the early 1960s, the United States had guaranteed a high price for each year's sugar harvest. But the dollars this brought in soon left the island again, to pay for capital goods, machinery and all the consumer items imported from the United States. This vicious circle mostly benefited U.S. capital and the small number of landowners and importers/exporters established in Cuba. Very little of the sugar wealth found its way back to the peasants, who had no land of their own and were largely employed seasonally. Nor did the sugar industry act as a spur for the development of other national industries, as the small number of Cuban entrepreneurs preferred to invest in real estate or to keep their dollars abroad.

Paradoxically, it had been Batista himself who in the mid-1950s had tried to lessen Cuba's dependence on this single commodity. His attempts to diversify in agriculture had largely failed, and now by the end of the 1960s Fidel Castro had also returned to placing his faith almost exclusively in the island's sugar exports. Perhaps owing to his rural background, he had always been more interested in agriculture than industry. Attempts to develop national manufacturing had largely been promoted by Che Guevara when he was the Minister of Industry, but by the second half of the 1960s Fidel and his closest associates believed that for Cuba to build up sufficient foreign reserves to enable it to launch into the kind of modernizing efforts in industry and infrastructure that had so far stubbornly refused to materialize, sugar exports were the key. The revenues from this would no longer be controlled by foreign concerns or self-interested individuals, but would come to the state, which would then disburse them in the most effective manner possible to stimulate the Cuban economy, as well as paying for the free education, health system and other social gains of the Revolution. In 1970, as outlined in the five-year plan for 1965–70, Castro set Cubans the task of producing a record ten million tons of sugar to sell to the Communist bloc of countries. He declared that this would solve the island's economic problems at a stroke. He also saw it as a means of galvanising the population, which was showing increasing signs of tiring of the constant efforts demanded by the government for what seemed like very little reward. In October 1969 he went so far as to write in *Granma*:

> The ten million ton harvest represents far more than tons of sugar, far more than an economic victory; it is a test, a moral commitment for this country. And precisely because it is a test and a moral commitment we cannot fall short by even a single gram of these ten million tons . . . Ten million tons less a single pound – we declare it before all the world – will be a defeat, not a victory.[8]

In the end, the sugar harvest of 1970 was more than a few grams short, even though it was a record 8.5 million tons, double that of the previous year. On the anniversary of the Moncada Barracks attack on 26 July 1970, Castro faced up to the public, and admitted that he and the other leaders of the Revolution had perhaps been too ambitious in what they had thought they could achieve in ten years. Reflecting on the struggle to build a new, revolutionary society in Cuba, he referred back to the Moncada Barracks and the time in the sierra, and concluded:

It is easier to win twenty wars than win the battle of development. The fight today is not against people – unless they are
ourselves – we are fighting against objective factors; we are
fighting against the past, we are fighting with the continued
presence of that past in the present, we are fighting against limi-
tations of all kinds. But sincerely this is the greatest challenge
that we have had in our lives, and the greatest challenge the
Revolution has ever faced.[9]

Although during this speech Castro offered to resign, his audience and the rest of Cuban society knew by now that he had no
intention of stepping down. His answer was to align Cuba even
more closely with Moscow. In the wake of the sugar harvest failure,
he replaced his economic advisers with people more closely aligned
to orthodox Communist thinking. In December 1970 a joint commission was set up with the Soviet Union to channel Russian aid.
Soviet economic and technical experts began to flood into Cuba,
advising on everything from military matters to industry and agriculture. In July 1972, Cuba joined COMECON (Council for Mutual
Economic Assistance), the economic grouping of Communist countries. By 1973, two-thirds of Cuban trade was with the Soviet Union.
The USSR had little interest in encouraging Cuba to develop its own
industry, or even to diversify in agriculture or reduce its reliance on
export crops in favour of self-sufficiency. In a similar way to what
had happened years earlier with the island's dollar earnings and
the United States, the currency now gained through the sale of
sugar to the Russians had to be spent in the eastern bloc. The
result was that Cuba's economic production became ever more
dependent on input from there. Throughout the 1970s and early
1980s, Cuba increasingly became another Soviet satellite.

Following the new thinking in Moscow, in Cuba material
incentives and wage differentials were brought in to try to resolve
the problem of low productivity, leading to the abandonment of

Che's attempts to stimulate production by moral exhortation and the power of example. One of the promises of the Revolution had been to guarantee employment for everyone. Over the years, this meant that many work-places were over-staffed, with those employed there having little to do, and little incentive to make any great effort. However, no serious attempts were introduced to make production in the state-run enterprises more responsive to demand: needs were determined following political criteria, and targets for production set accordingly.

In the mid-1970s Castro also moved to establish more permanent political institutions to replace the often ad hoc system that had grown out of the rebel victory. This led to what was called the 'first socialist constitution' in February 1976, which provided for a new legal code and the establishment of state institutions. Under its provisions, Marxism-Leninism was enshrined as the state ideology. There was to be a single head of state and government, and the Communist Party of Cuba was recognized as the only authorized political party. The new constitution also brought in what is known as *poder popular* (popular power) – the discussion and channelling of different points of view into official institutions at the municipal, provincial and national levels. At the local level, approved candidates were chosen by secret ballot. December 1976 saw the inaugural meeting of the first National Assembly formed by these new elected representatives, where input from below is meant to be debated and then presented to the Council of Ministers, the next tier up in the decision-making process. Above them in the Council of State, whose president and vice-president (Fidel and his brother Raúl Castro respectively from 1976 to 2008) are elected by the members of the National Assembly. The National Assembly also elects the judiciary. The British academic Jean Stubbs, who has studied the Cuban political system for many years, concludes:

Cuba is undeniably a one-party state, but within the system there are channels for non-party participation. This participatory mechanism functions better at the community level and less well when it comes to national decision-making levels.[10]

In many ways, this institutionalization of the Revolution was a recognition that the spirit of the 1960s was definitely a thing of the past, that mass voluntary efforts could no longer be relied on to carry the Revolution forward (once again, the lesson of the 1970 sugar harvest failure) and that some kind of representative system needed to be put in place instead.

At the same time, the new material incentives and wage differentials, with 'advanced workers' earning considerably more than others, meant that Cuban society became increasingly stratified. Those managers (loyal Communist Party members) and other 'advanced' workers began to see benefits such as cars, a greater ability to purchase consumer goods, and perhaps most importantly, greater access to the still woefully scarce possibility of decent housing. After all this process of institutionalization, Fidel Castro was even more firmly in charge of the decision-making process: he was now commander-in-chief of the armed forces, first secretary of the Communist party, and president of the Council of State and of the council of ministers. Although the system was theoretically designed for ideas and legislative proposals to percolate upwards from the grass-roots level, all too often it worked in the opposite direction, with Fidel's personal agenda being transferred downwards for implementation by people who were never consulted in the first place.

The 1970s also saw Fidel looking to make his mark on a larger stage than Cuba. Some biographers such as Tad Szulc have seen this as little more than boredom;[11] others that as he was relieved of some of the pressures of daily routine within Cuba, he saw the best way of defending his regime as making sure it had a voice on a larger stage. So it was that he made sure Cuba played a prominent part in the emergence of the Non-Aligned Movement, of which he was elected president in 1979. He was also convinced of the revolutionary potential in the emerging countries of Africa, despite Guevara's dismal failure in the Congo. He began to travel there, and to build up Cuban influence in the local communist parties. Beyond that, he started to commit Cuban soldiers to offer direct help. From 1975 onwards, Cuban troops fought in Angola alongside António Agostinho Neto's MPLA forces. In his *Operación Carlota*, García Márquez explained why this was so important:

> even Cubans who did not feel passionately about it felt compensated by life after many years of unjust setbacks. In 1970, when the 10 million tonne sugar harvest was a failure, Fidel Castro asked the people to turn defeat into victory. In fact, the Cuban people had been doing that for far too long with stubborn political awareness and cast-iron moral fortitude. Ever since victory at the Bay of Pigs, fifteen years earlier, they had been forced to accept, with gritted teeth, the murders of Che Guevara in Bolivia and of President Salvador Allende in the Chilean catastrophe, they had suffered with the annihilation of the guerrillas in Latin America, the unending night of the U.S. blockade, and the hidden, implacable eating away of so many past mistakes that more than once led them to the verge of disaster. All this, despite the irreversible but slow and hard-won victories of the Revolution, must have created a growing sense of undeserved penances forced on them. Angola at last offered them the gratification of the great victory they needed so much.[12]

The Cubans were credited with not only helping Neto avoid defeat, but with driving South African forces out of the country and helping him to declare independence. However, it was not until 1991, and after important battles such as Cuito Cuanavale in

1988, that the last Cuban troops left Angola. By this time some 2,000 soldiers had been killed, and a further 10,000 wounded. The Cuban forces returned home as heroes, but as in other countries, many of the former soldiers found it hard to re-adapt to life after combat, while Castro eventually came to see their commanders as a threat, and a few years later dealt with them in drastic fashion, as outlined in the following chapter. Cuba also intervened in the Horn of Africa, when in 1977 some 17,000 Cuban troops helped the forces of the 'socialist' officers in charge in Ethiopia ward off an invasion attempt by troops from Somalia, despite the fact that Cuba had previously supported the latter country. The Cuban forces remained to help prop up the Mengistu regime in Addis Ababa for a further 12 years, before pulling out completely in 1989.

Within Latin America, Cuba and Castro continued to offer training, finance, and logistical support to armed rebel groups aiming to topple repressive regimes. In 1970, it seemed as though socialism had finally taken hold on the Latin American mainland, when the Socialist party leader Salvador Allende was elected president in Chile. Allende had visited Cuba several times, and he and Castro got on well personally, but Fidel had doubts about the Chilean leader's attempts to usher in a socialist revolution by the 'parliamentary road'. Castro expressed his reservations during a long stay he made in Chile towards the end of 1971, and was proved right in September 1973 when the political and social divisions in the country led to the bloody takeover led by General Augusto Pinochet and the military junta (and Allende's suicide, apparently with bullets from a gun Fidel Castro had given him). In Che's native Argentina, and in Uruguay and Brazil, young radicals looked to the example of the Cuban Revolution and attempted to repeat its success. The results were predictably disastrous, and provoked a reaction from the Right and the military which led to repression on a scale not seen in many years. It was in the smaller, less developed countries of Central America that the left-wing revolutionaries were more successful. In Nicaragua, the

Sandinistas led a popular revolt against the Somoza dynasty that had many echoes of the Cuban struggle against Batista. In July 1979 the Sandinistas overthrew the Somoza regime and took power. They were almost immediately faced with armed opposition, once again largely financed by the USA. But this was not a liberation struggle in distant Africa, and although Castro offered support and sent advisers to Managua, he was careful not to commit any troops. Similarly in El Salvador, where a civil war that pitted the rebel forces of the FMLN (Farabundo Martí National Liberation Front) against the right-wing regime and the armed forces, Castro encouraged the revolutionaries to organize from Cuba, but did not send any combat troops into what eventually proved to be a losing struggle.

By now in his forties, by the end of the 1970s Fidel Castro had succeeded in establishing a revolution that the British historian Eric Hobsbawm described as a 'global concept'.[13] In many ways, this was due to his force of character, and the persuasiveness of his oratorical style. Castro most of all enjoyed making unscripted speeches to huge crowds who were there in front of him. The French philosopher Jean-Paul Sartre was one of the first to provide a description of Castro's rhetorical style. Sartre was present at the funeral oration Castro gave early in 1960 for the victims of the sabotage of the *La Coubre* munitions ship in Havana harbour (an event that was also to produce the iconic image of a furious Che Guevara in beret and leather jacket). His words could be applied to thousands of similar speeches made by the Cuban leader:

It is hard to transmit the restlessness, the groping, the stops, the brusque beginnings, the slowness and then the progressive acceleration of the delivery, and above all, under the bubbling of anger, the application of this almost sad honesty, that curious marriage of the most fierce resolution with the almost timid, conscientious desire to do well. These words were steps. With each, one advanced a little farther – irreversibly.[14]

The subject of his speech was often a policy decision that he had made alone, or with his closest advisers. The purpose of him speaking was to convince his audience that they too were involved in making this particular choice, and more than that – they had participated in it. To do this, Castro set out what for him were the incontrovertible facts – whether it be about dairy production in Cuba, the anti-imperialist struggle in Vietnam or Venezuela, the sugar harvest, and so on. To give weight to the facts or situation he wished to outline, he first gave the information quite quickly, but then paused, and repeated it several times, so that its importance would sink in. After this, he linked the first fact with the next, again stopping to underline how this followed logically from the previous one. Often, the right forefinger wass raised high in the air to emphasize the point. At other times, when he was thinking out loud, the finger was lower, by his side, and crooked. At critical junctures, he would ask for the crowd's answer to a question he had just posed – once again, bringing them closer to him and persuading them they were part of the decision-making process.

Other observers have thought they could trace Castro's obsessive, insistent reasoning back to his early education with the Jesuits. Once again, it is his writer friend Gabriel García Márquez who has best traced the way that a topic gradually mades its way to become a theme for a public speech:

> The subject of Latin America's foreign debt, for example, had arisen in his conversations for the first time some two years ago, and had been developing, branching out, growing more profound, until it became something very much like a recurrent nightmare. The first thing he said, like a simple arithmetical conclusion, was that the debt was unpayable. Little by little, during three trips I made to Havana that year, I pieced together his latest variations on the themes: the repercussions of the debt on the countries' economies, its political and social impact, its

Castro in typical stance addressing a crowd in the mid-1960s.

decisive influence on international relations, its providential importance for a unitary Latin American policy. Finally, he convoked a major congress of experts in Havana and gave a speech in which he left out none of the salient questions from his preceding conversations. By then he had a comprehensive vision which only the passage of time will bear out.[15]

The problems of this kind of rhetorical style are obvious. Above all, Fidel Castro's speeches on anything and everything rarely lasted less than several hours. As he outlined the thought processes described by García Márquez, his listeners had to sit, or more usually stand, in the heat or the discomfort of parades. In the end, it was this inveterate habit of endless public speaking which led at least in part to Castro's downfall. It was in June 2001 that he almost fainted on an extremely hot day as he was preparing to make a long speech. This was the first time that many Cubans had any inkling that their leader might be growing old, and was mortal just like everyone else.

The other great problem of Castro's oratory was that no one else was allowed to get a word in. Although he may have discussed matters such as Latin America's debt with experts, his was always the final word. Very rarely was anyone allowed to interrupt or contradict his opinions, however lengthily and tediously he may have propounded them. This is not the oratory of debate, but of authoritarianism, and is especially dangerous when a single individual claims to have expert knowledge of every subject under the sun. As ever, the greatest danger comes when the person claiming this knowledge comes to believe it himself, and does not merely set out proposals, but is in a position to put them into practice. The history of Cuba under Castro is littered with countless ideas and schemes which he became convinced were of vital importance to the nation: from the 'ten million ton' record sugar harvest of 1970, to the idea of promoting Cuba as a great cheese producer.

In the 1970s, Fidel Castro's rhetorical power won a great deal of support among the newly emerging nations of Africa and Asia. Back in Cuba however, his constant calls for more efforts and greater sacrifices were beginning to wear thin with a populace that had become accustomed to the social benefits offered by the regime, but increasingly hoped for greater material improvements in their daily lives as well. Fidel might continue to insist that 'we have something more powerful than money, and that is conscience', or again that 'a communist is more powerful than a capitalist, because he is not for sale',[16] but as events were soon to show, a significant portion of the Cuban people was not so convinced.

6

Losing the Plot

The four years of Jimmy Carter's presidency at the end of the 1970s led to a thaw in relations between the regime in Cuba and Washington. In *My Life*, Castro says he always

> had a high opinion of Carter as a man of honour, an ethical man. His policies towards Cuba were constructive, and he was one of [the United States'] most honest presidents.[1]

One example of this more constructive approach saw the two countries establish 'Interests' offices in their respective capitals, which led to permission for Cuban exiles to visit their families back in Cuba, and to bring u.s. dollars with them. This turned out to be a near-disaster for the Castro regime: the glimpses these visitors offered of a very different world just across the Florida Straits were enough to upset the fragile equilibrium on the island. In April 1980 a bus load of Cubans smashed their way into the Peruvian embassy in Havana. Thousands more followed, until eventually Castro allowed boats from Florida to come and pick up all those who wanted to leave from the port of Mariel. At the same time he emptied prisons and mental hospitals, while 'repudiation committees' forced out many others who were considered to have 'counter-revolutionary' tendencies. As many as 125,000 Cubans left before President Carter closed the loophole at the end of September 1980, fearing that the flood of immigrants would harm his re-election efforts. Although Castro claimed that this exodus had been a good way of 'cleansing the revolution', the level of discontent it showed among people who for the most part were ordinary Cubans was hardly a good advertisement for a revolution that had been in power for more than two decades.[2] Although Fidel once more tried to suggest he had somehow scored a notable victory over the United States by exporting the 'undesirables' from Cuba, he was undoubtedly shocked that as many as one million Cubans wanted to sign up for a way out of the island.

Several of the Cuban leader's biographers have suggested that Fidel's unusually hesitant dealing with this crisis was due at least in part to the illness and death from cancer of his long-standing companion, Celia Sánchez. According to reports from sources close to the Cuban leader, her loss in 1980 affected him so deeply that he lost touch with what was going on in the island for months. The fact that this was never more than a rumour reflects the secrecy that has surrounded his life since he came to power in 1959. In fact, Fidel Castro has been twice married and has fathered at least eight children. His first marriage to Mirta, the daughter of the rich Díaz-Balart clan, took place on 12 October 1948, when he was 22 and already deeply involved in student politics. Despite the birth of their son Fidelito the following year, Mirta had little interest in her husband's political activities with the Partido Ortodoxo: her own family were closely involved with the Batista regime. But it was after the 1953 attack on the Moncada Barracks that Mirta became aware of the liaison Fidel had with Natalia (Naty) Revuelta. Naty was a beautiful socialite in early 1950s Havana. Like many others, she was revolted by the repression and gangsterism of the Batista regime. She became a fervent supporter of the opposition Ortodoxo Party, and in 1953 she and Fidel began their relationship, when both of them were married to other people. Naty even pawned some of her jewels to finance the opposition, and distributed the manifesto for the would-be revolutionaries. After Fidel's imprisonment, the two began a passionate correspondence. When he was amnestied in 1955, the pair continued their romance. By this time Fidel was divorced from Mirta, but Naty was still married to the eminent physician Orlando Fernández. On 19 March 1956 she gave birth to Alina, Fidel's daughter. A photograph of Alina's baptism some time later shows a formal ceremony, with Naty radiant in a white gown and matching handbag, while Orlando Fernández stares expressionless at the camera as he contemplates the cuckoo in the marital nest.[3]

Fernández divorced his wife not long afterwards, but Fidel was by then in exile in Mexico and subsequently fighting in the Sierra Maestra mountains, something which did not appeal to the Naty Havana sophisticate. Their relationship soon foundered. Their daughter Alina struggled with life in Cuba for almost 40 years, trying to come to terms with who her father was. She was expected to be an exemplary revolutionary, when what she wanted most of all was a father who would not only officially recognize her existence, but come to visit her and give her individual attention. With many more children of his own to look after, Fidel never did come with any regularity. In 1993 Alina left Cuba, first for Madrid and later for Miami. Mirta Díaz-Balart left the island much earlier. After her divorce in 1954 she headed for the United States with their five-year-old son, Fidelito. The next few years saw a fierce tussle over which of the two should have custody of the boy, until in 1959 he went back to Cuba, just in time to join the victory ride into Havana on a captured Batista tank. Later, he was sent to study physics in the Soviet Union, and from 1980 to 1992 was the head of the Cuban nuclear energy programme. This has been a notorious failure, with the plants at Juragua near Cienfuegos on the northwest coast designed and built by the Soviets never coming on-stream. In fact, Fidelito performed so badly in this that his father had him sacked, commenting, 'There was no resignation. He was fired for incompetence. We don't have a monarchy here.'[4] Despite this humiliation, he later returned as a professor of nuclear physics at the Cuban Academy of Science. When her young son was first taken back to Havana, Mirta stayed there too, but in the late 1960s managed to get out and went to live in Madrid. According to Ann Louise Bardach, she still visited her son in Cuba, but it was not until around the year 2000, thanks apparently to the efforts of Raúl Castro, that there was a reconciliation between her and Fidel. (Following his near-fatal illness in 2006, Mirta returned to live in Havana with her son Fidelito's family.)

It was following the defeat of the Batista regime and the installation of the revolutionary government that Fidel Castro met the woman who bore him five sons, although, as in his father's case, he did not marry her until after they were all born. Dalia Soto del Valle was a teacher from Trinidad, a town in the south of the island. The daughter of a wealthy cigarette factory owner, she is not known to have participated in the guerrilla war or to have any great political interests. She has never played any public role, and is not introduced at public events. In fact, it was not until the first decade of the twenty-first century that the official media in Cuba began to recognize her existence and show her on news footage. Throughout the 1960s she was busy bearing children: Alexis was born in 1963; then Alexander in 1965; Alejandro in 1967; Antonio in 1968 and Angel in 1974. Naming his last son after his father was possibly Fidel's nod to the founder of the dynasty, perhaps also a wish to prove he could be equally productive when it came to having children. As well as these seven recognized children, some writers are convinced that Fidel has fathered at least three or four more in short relationships. Fidel himself once declared modestly it was 'less than a dozen'.[5]

Whatever the truth about the turmoil in Castro's private life, with Jimmy Carter's electoral defeat and the arrival of the hawkish Ronald Reagan to the u.s. presidency in 1981, relations between the two countries were once more on a collision course. According to Robert Macfarlane, u.s. National Security Advisor in the 1980s, some of the Reagan team even considered a fresh initiative against Castro:

> Secretary of State Haig believed that trying to pressure Castro and to bring down the executive of Cuba was a worthwhile goal . . . He wanted to start with a bang.[6]

For Reagan, Cuba was part of the 'axis of evil', and although in the end there was no direct attempt to invade the island, it was in October 1983 during his first term in office that u.s. forces and Cuban troops exchanged shots directly for the first and only time.

This was when u.s. forces invaded the tiny Caribbean island of Grenada, where Cuban personnel had been building a new airport and offering armed support to the 'revolutionary' government led by Maurice Bishop. After Bishop was executed by a splinter group within the New Jewel Movement, it was almost inevitable that Washington would intervene. Some 7,000 u.s. marines were sent in, and they met with determined resistance from Grenadian and Cuban units. According to some reports, as many as 29 Cubans were killed, and another 600 were eventually repatriated.

Reagan also did all he could to topple the pro-Cuban Sandinista regime in Nicaragua. He used Cuban exiles as intermediaries in the purchase of weapons to supply the 'Contras' or counter-revolution-aries in that country, so that the Sandinistas found themselves caught up in a costly war that prevented them making progress towards the ambitious social goals that their Revolution had prom-ised. It was also pressure from the United States that then led President Ortega to hold elections in 1989, which the Sandinistas lost. Fidel Castro for his part sent advisers and medical doctors to Nicaragua, but refused to commit troops there. He also strongly advised the Sandinista government not to agree to elections when Nicaragua was so deeply divided: his experience and instinct once more proved him right. In El Salvador too, the Reagan administration poured in funds to prop up the right-wing government challenged by the FMLN guerrillas (backed by Havana). Again, this huge investment paid off, but only after some 75,000 people out of a total population of less than three million had been killed or 'disappeared'.

In Cuba itself, the Mariel boatlift had shown Castro and the rest of the leadership that a significant proportion of the population was unhappy with the results of the Revolution, especially among the young people who had never known anything different. They had not seen the injustices of the pre-revolutionary era, but nor had they seen the early days of revolutionary promise of the 1960s. Many of them questioned why daily life was still such a struggle, and why their lives seemed to hold out such little hope of change for the better – in material terms, but also with regard to freedom of movement and opportunities.

After more than 25 years in power, the revolutionary government had brought improvements in many areas. According to official figures, life expectancy had increased from 57 to 74, while the infant mortality rate had dropped from 60 per 1,000 births to a little more than 13 per 1,000. The number of doctors and medical personnel, especially in the previously neglected rural areas, had increased tenfold. All children went at least to primary school, and levels of illiteracy had fallen dramatically. But with these basic needs being met, many Cubans chafed at the lack of freedom to move around the island or to go abroad. They wanted more goods in the shops, and a wider range of foodstuffs to purchase beyond what their ration books offered.

The Cuban economy was struggling. Growth fell while the government's budget deficit increased, so that in 1985 it was unable to service its international debt. Low productivity, the inflexibility of central planning, and bureaucratic inefficiency and corruption all compounded the problem. The continued hostility of the Reagan administration and the U.S. trade embargo only served to make things worse. In response, the first half of the 1980s had seen some timid attempts to allow a market system and small private sector, reluctantly agreed to by Fidel. Farm produce could be sold at markets; individuals could register to provide services such as plumbing, car repairs, handicrafts and so on outside the state sector. A 1985 law giving tenants the right to buy the state-provided housing they were living in rapidly created a private market that led to an increase in the value of property, especially in Havana. The law was soon repealed, and the decision was taken not to allow any more similar loosening of state control.

Instead, in 1986 Castro began what he called a process of 'rectification of errors and negative trends'. This process put a brake on any opening to the market, reinforced central control of the economy, and sought to restrict consumer imports still further. This was accompanied by an effort to re-awaken the moral commitment of the Cuban people: again and again in his speeches of the period Fidel stressed that is was solidarity and a lack of selfishness that distinguished the islanders from the capitalist world, and that the profit motive had no place in his Cuba. For example, he blamed the massive absenteeism and low productivity obvious throughout the island's industries on leftover 'capitalist habits' and 'selfishness' that had not yet been eradicated. In a speech to the Third Communist Party Congress in February 1986, he explicitly contrasted the Cuban system with capitalism:

> Capitalists who manage to survive competition are demanding, very demanding, or else they do not survive. Where there's no competition, if the motivation prompting the owner in a capitalist society to defend his personal interests is out of the question, what is there to substitute? Only the cadres' individual sense of responsibility, the role played by cadres . . . A consciousness, a revolutionary will and vocation, were,

are, and always will be a thousand times more powerful than money.[7]

He also obliquely acknowledged the problems of the lack of choice and consumer goods, only to dismiss the question with the customary appeal to the future:

To tell the truth, we would like ten or twenty metres more of cloth per capita, but that is not our problem at the moment; our problem is development, our problem is the future. We can't mortgage the future for ten metres of cloth![8]

Again, during a speech to mark the twentieth anniversary of Che Guevara's death on 8 October 1987, he continued to stress that he was trying to restore a sense of revolutionary values into the flagging Cuban system:

Rectification is not idealism, but realism, better use of the economic and planning system . . . what are we rectifying? We're rectifying all those things – and there are many – that strayed from the revolutionary spirit, from revolutionary work, revolutionary virtue, revolutionary effort, revolutionary responsibility; all those things that strayed from the spirit of solidarity among people. We're rectifying all the shoddiness and mediocrity that is precisely the negation of Che's ideas, his revolutionary thought, his style, his spirit and his example.

The voluntary 'micro-brigades' that had been widespread in the 1960s were brought in once more to build new homes and bring in the sugar harvest. At the same time, the government introduced measures designed to save energy, raised transport prices, and reduced the amount of food available on ration books. Once more,

With Mikhail Gorbachev in Havana, mid-1980s.

Cubans were being asked to make personal sacrifices in the name of ideology.

In other parts of the world, this ideology was being challenged from within. On 11 March 1985, Mikhail Gorbachev became General Secretary of the Communist Party in the USSR. Castro met him in February 1986, when the Soviet leader promised to continue the essential Soviet aid to the island. As the implications of his policies of *glasnost* and *perestroika* became clearer, however, the Cuban leader began to denounce them as dangerous and un-socialist. Gorbachev eventually visited Havana in April 1989. He made it clear that economic and military relations between the two countries would have to be put on a more realistic footing. The USSR had been buying most of Cuba's sugar each year at inflated prices, while supplying the island with oil and foodstuffs at heavily subsidized rates. The Soviet leader wanted market prices to be introduced, and for Soviet imports to be paid for in U.S. dollars.

The collapse of the communist governments in Eastern Europe in 1989, followed two years later by that of the Soviet Union itself, was regarded by Fidel Castro as proof that he had been right to resist moves towards greater liberalization in Cuba. Controlled 'rectification' was one thing, fundamental change to the system quite another. In his interviews with the editor of *Le Monde Diplomatique*, Ignacio Ramonet (later collected as *My Life*), Castro was dismissive of perestroika and immediately linked it, as ever, to the threat from the United States:

> If we'd had that perestroika, the Americans would have been delighted, because, as you know, the Soviets destroyed themselves. If we'd split into ten factions and a huge power struggle had started here, the Americans would have been the happiest people in the world; they'd have said, 'We're finally going to get rid of that Cuban Revolution down there.' If we'd started carrying out reforms like that, which have nothing to do with conditions in Cuba, we'd have destroyed ourselves. But we're not going to destroy ourselves – that needs to be very clear.[9]

As so often in the past, Castro took the new situation as a personal challenge, and flung himself into efforts to combat its dangers. He declared that Cuba had to face the fact that this was now a 'unipolar world', which meant it was in a 'special period in times of peace'. But no fine speeches could hide the disastrous economic situation: Cuba's GDP fell by some 35 per cent in the four years from 1989 to 1993, while exports fell by almost 80 per cent.[10] For ordinary Cubans, this meant yet more food rationing, more energy blackouts, the use of horses and bicycles rather than cars, and stricter surveillance to make sure that the waves of popular protest that had swept away the communist regimes in Eastern Europe did not erupt on the island.

In fact, it was in 1989 that perhaps one of the most serious challenges to Castro's rule had occurred. Without warning, it was suddenly announced that four top members of the Cuban armed forces had been arrested and were to be tried before a military court on charges of corruption and illegal drug smuggling. They were charged with illegal trading in diamonds and ivory from Angola in order to buy weapons and ammunition.[11] Even more seriously, they were accused of taking money from left-wing Colombian rebels (Revolutionary Armed Forces of Colombia – FARC) who wanted to use Cuban air space and territorial waters for running cocaine to the United States. The men claimed they were simply obtaining foreign currency to be used to bolster the state's coffers. Many exiles in Miami, and some members of the George H. W. Bush administration, speculated that this kind of high-level operation could only have been carried out with Fidel Castro's knowledge and approval, but no proof of this has as yet come to light. In the end, two of the high-ranking officers were executed, and two others given life sentences. One of those shot, General Arnaldo Ochoa, was a veteran of the Sierra Maestra campaign, a hero of the Cuban effort in Angola, and one of Raúl Castro's closest friends. He was also known as someone who had voiced criticism of the tightening of the regime ordered by Castro in response to events in the Soviet Union. The other man shot, the charismatic Colonel Antonio de la Guardia, had long been an important member of the Cuban intelligence services. Although no proof has ever been forthcoming, many observers in the United States

Greeting troops returning from Africa, 1990.

at least have suggested Castro might have been afraid of a coup orchestrated by these highly respected military men aimed at replacing him and his brother with more reform-minded leaders. As the Miami-based journalist Andrés Oppenheimer (author of the rather over-optimistic *Castro's Final Hour* in 1993) told me in an interview:

> Castro was seeing the Communist regimes falling one after the other and he wanted to send a strong message to his military that you're not gonna screw around with me. There can be no stronger message than executing some of your top aides, some of the most popular generals within the armed services.[12]

As usual, the party newspaper *Granma* published the official line in its editorial:

> Although extremely surprising and bitter for our people, these events demonstrate that although grave defects of a moral as

well as physical order can occur among individuals, in our country, absolutely nobody, no matter how great his merits, nor how high he may be in the hierarchy, can violate the laws and principles of the revolution with impunity.[13]

Whether this episode had really been a potential uprising against Fidel or not, there is no doubt that as the Revolution entered its fourth decade the challenges facing him and his government were as great as those that had arisen at any time since the guerrilla victory at the end of 1958. As in the past, the Cuban leader took these difficulties as a personal test, and once more deliberately placed himself centre stage. By now he was in his mid-sixties, and the thought of handing over any power or responsibility to a younger generation does not seem to have even remotely occurred to him.

7

The Special Period

Although this apparent challenge to his leadership from some high-ranking members of the armed forces was snuffed out, the early 1990s were yet another testing time for Fidel. At first, as he told the National Assembly in 1989, he was unsure about the impact that Gorbachev's reforms would have for the Soviet Union and for Cuba:

> Reforms are taking place in the socialist camp, especially the USSR. If they're successful, it will be good for socialism and for us all. If they run into serious difficulties, the consequences will be hard, especially for us. We can expect difficulties from the enemy camp and difficulties that might come from our own friends. But not even that should discourage us.[1]

The ensuing rapid collapse of the Soviet communist party and then of the Soviet Union itself seems to have taken him and his closest associates by surprise. Castro's answer was to insist still further on the core values of revolutionary solidarity and central-ized state planning to oversee production and distribution. Early in 1990, Castro officially announced what he called 'The Special Period in Times of Peace'. This was a desperate attempt to survive in the most adverse conditions: without the guaranteed markets for sugar, citrus fruits, tobacco and other products in the communist bloc, the country's exports collapsed. Equally, there was little foreign currency to pay for imports, which soon fell to less than half of what they had been in the 1980s. As a result, Cuba was soon facing an increasingly crippling trade deficit, which the government had to make up through international loans that were far less generous than when their Soviet allies had been supporting them. Fidel therefore announced cuts in public spending and reductions in food subsidies and items on the ration cards. In Havana and other cities electricity was also cut back, as was the already parlous public transport system. For the countryside, Fidel extolled the virtues of '*tracción a sangre*' ('animal power'), meaning the use of oxen and horses rather than tractors that wasted expensive fuel.

These new crisis measures were debated at the much-delayed Fourth Party Congress in 1991. The Communist party was recognized as the one official political party on the island, although it was now called 'the party of the Cuban nation' rather than the 'party of the working class'. Cuba was also no longer described as an 'atheist' state, and Catholics and other religious believers were now allowed to become party members. In addition, the Congress saw the start of a process of ideological re-alignment which lessened the importance of figures such as Marx or Lenin in favour of national heroes such as José Martí and the other nineteenth-century heroes of the independence struggle. From now on, influential figures in the regime such as Minister of Culture Armando Hart were keen to emphasize that the 1959 Revolution was a continuation of that tradition, rather than a result of exogenous ideas. Rather than quoting Marx, they increasingly harked back to the independence struggle begun by the *mambises* in the 1860s, or the fight against the Machado regime of the early 1930s.[2]

The 1991 Congress also provided the opportunity for those in the communist party who advocated reforms similar to perestroika, led by Foreign Minister Carlos Aldana, to make their voices heard. They called for the introduction of market mechanisms to regulate prices, but more importantly, for the creation of other political parties alongside the communist party. Their reform proposals were largely rejected, and a year later Aldana himself was removed from office and replaced with a hardliner who had once been the Cuban Ambassador in Moscow.

However, the economic crisis was by now so great that something drastic had to be attempted. This came in 1993 with the legalization of the use of the u.s. dollar in Cuba (there had been a huge black market in dollars for years) and permission for small individual *cuentapropista* (self-employed) businesses to operate. Joint ventures with foreign companies were encouraged; as a result, foreign capital gave a huge boost mainly to the tourist industry, with new hotels and facilities springing up in many places. The Cuban state was anxious to get its hands on some hard currency, but the measures only served to increase the disparities between Cubans who had access to funds from members of their family living in exile and those who had to make do with Cuban pesos. As Sebastian Balfour outlines, by the mid-1990s

> Cuba had four different economies, a thriving black economy providing some 60 per cent of the population's basic food needs, an independent, enclave export sector, a hard currency consumer market open to those with dollars, and a nationalised economy marked by low productivity and severe rationing and reliant to a great extent on voluntary work.[3]

In 1993 Castro had told the National Assembly that 'we have the right to invent things to survive in these conditions without ever ceasing to be revolutionaries.' In a typical display of Cuban humour, when people on the street were asked how they managed, they often replied *'inventando'* – 'inventing' ways to survive. However, there were increasing signs in 1993–4 that the patience of ordinary Cubans had reached breaking point. Thousands took the drastic measure of launching themselves into the Florida Straits on makeshift embarkations in a desperate attempt to reach the United States. So many of these '*balseros*' (rafters) arrived in Florida that the recently elected president Bill Clinton quickly signed an agreement with the Cuban authorities that allowed for 20,000 visas to be granted annually to Cubans wishing to emigrate, but stipulating that all *balseros* intercepted at sea would be returned to Cuba. More worryingly still for Fidel and the Cuban authorities was the fact that in the stiflingly hot summer of 1994 there was real hunger in the cities, and serious unrest on the streets of Havana. As ever, Castro himself took the lead, going into the streets and personally trying to calm things down. Many Cubans still had enormous respect for him, and blamed the country's problems on mismanagement by the bureaucrats beneath him, so that the situation gradually settled, although widespread discontent continued to simmer.

Despite the arrival of Clinton in the White House in 1992, there was no improvement in relations with the United States. If anything, they became even more strained. In late 1992, the U.S. trade embargo with the island was tightened still further by means of the Torricelli Amendment or more grandly, the Cuban Democracy Act. This imposed strict controls on relatives sending dollars back to family members in Cuba, and banned U.S. companies and subsidiaries based outside the United States from trading with the island. This was followed up in 1996 by the equally grandiose Cuban Liberty and Democratic Solidarity Act, also known as the Helms–Burton Bill. The act threatened reprisals against any countries, institutions or companies that provided loans to Cuba or did business there. Britain and the EU protested that this was illegal under international law, and both President Clinton and his successor in the White House, George W. Bush, repeatedly signed waivers suspending the legislation. However, several U.S. firms operating abroad were fined under its provisions, and the act operated as yet another brake on foreign trade with the island.[4]

The Helms-Burton Bill was passed by the U.S. Congress in the wake of another dangerous flare-up in relations between the two countries. The Cuban exile group *Hermanos al Rescate* (Brothers to the Rescue) was originally formed to provide aircraft that could patrol and help rescue any Cubans crossing the Florida Straits. But it soon began dropping anti-Castro leaflets and other propaganda over Havana, until 24 February 1996, when two of its planes were shot down by Cuban fighters, apparently in international air space.

The Cuban exiles in Miami and other parts of the United States were by now more than a million strong. The vast majority of them, particularly among the older generations, were stridently opposed to the Castro regime, and although the U.S. government kept the pledge made by President Kennedy in 1962 not to attempt to invade the island, some of the exiles took the matter into their own hands. There were many isolated incidents of sabotage in the 1970s and 1980s, and some of the extremists saw the crisis after the withdrawal of the Soviet Union as an opportunity to step up their campaign. Two among them have become notorious for their efforts over the decades to eliminate Castro in person, as well as to attack his regime at every possible opportunity, no matter what the cost in lives.

Orlando Bosch studied medicine at the University of Havana in the late 1940s, when Castro was studying law and taking his first steps in politics. Bosch also became a student leader, and moved into open opposition to the Batista dictatorship. He joined the rebel forces in 1958, fighting with Che Guevara's men in the central Las Villas province. After the revolutionary victory, he was briefly put in charge of the province, but quickly split from Castro and Guevara and began an armed revolt against the new regime. When the revolt was crushed, Bosch moved to Miami, only eighteen months after the Revolution, in July 1960.

In Miami, in addition to setting up as a paediatrician, Bosch staged a personal war against Fidel Castro and his regime, characterized by bombings and assassinations, which he regarded as legitimate acts of war. He spent almost twenty years in prison in the United States and Venezuela on terrorism-related charges. In the 1960s he founded a group known as 'Cuban Power',[5] which carried out attacks in Cuba and the United States. It was in 1968 after he had tried to blow up a Polish freighter bound for Cuba that Bosch was arrested and served his first lengthy jail sentence. Bosch was also at the root of much of the violence that broke out between the anti-Castro groups in Miami in the mid-1970s, but before he could be arrested and charged with any of the killings, he decamped to Venezuela.

In 1976 he made another attempt to bring the various anti-Castro factions together in the CORU (Co-ordination of United Revolutionary Organizations). He allegedly called for the group to demonstrate its capacity by staging a major attack on the Cuban regime: shortly afterwards, in October 1976, Cubana de Aviación flight 455 was blown up over the Caribbean, killing 73 people, including 24 members of the Cuban national fencing team. Bosch has always maintained that this was a legitimate target, as 'all Castro's planes are warplanes'. He was arrested in Venezuela together with Luis Posada Carriles and two others. He again spent several years in jail waiting to be tried, before being acquitted in 1986.

When he arrived back in Miami in 1988, Bosch was detained for illegal entry and breaking the terms of his earlier parole. He was released in 1990, following a campaign on his behalf by aspiring Republican senator Ileana Ros-Lehtinen (whose campaign manager was none other than Jeb Bush, son of then serving president, George H. W. Bush). After his release, Orlando Bosch lived quietly in Miami, apparently having renounced violence. He died there in 2011.[6] When Fidel Castro's health gave out in 2006, he told a Spanish newspaper that he was 'frustrated. I would have liked to kill that man to set an example for future generations. The prospect that he will die in bed really upsets me.'[7] Three years later, the Cuban newspaper *Granma* returned the compliment, when the incoming Obama administration did nothing to press charges against Bosch:

> months after the administration change in Washington, nothing seems to have changed in the banana republic where the monstrous Orlando Bosch, the pediatrician killer, sleeps peacefully in his bed.[8]

Bosch's alleged co-conspirator in the 1976 airliner bombing, Luis Posada Carriles, has if anything been an even more fervent practitioner of direct action against the Cuban leader and his regime. When Fidel Castro came to power in 1959 he was almost immediately opposed to the new government, and set out on a campaign of violence against it. Helped directly by the CIA, he undertook acts of sabotage in Havana until, in January 1961, he had to seek asylum in the embassy of Argentina and then return to Miami via Mexico. He arrived just in time to sign up for the Bay of Pigs invasion attempt. When that failed, Posada Carriles was among the two hundred or so Cuban exiles signed up by the CIA for 'officer training' in covert operations. From then on, as his own defence lawyers have frequently asserted, he was a CIA 'paid asset'.

Even more than Orlando Bosch, Posada Carriles saw the elimination of Fidel Castro as his primary goal. He has reputedly been involved in assassination attempts, from Fidel Castro's visit to President Salvador Allende's Chile in 1971 to the Ibero-American summit in Panama in the year 2000. He was closely involved in the 1976 downing of the Cubana airliner, and was arrested together with Bosch and the other two suspects. Since he had taken Venezuelan citizenship, Posada Carriles was worried that his position was considerably weaker than theirs as foreigners, and so in 1985 he escaped from detention after bribing the prison governor.[9]

Posada Carriles soon found himself in El Salvador, where he became part of the operation running guns to the Contra forces fighting the revolutionary Sandinista government in nearby Nicaragua. Once again he was on the CIA payroll. After the Iran-Contra scandal broke, he continued to live in Central America and went on with his anti-communist campaigns. His name became prominent once more in 1997, when he was linked to a series of bombings in Cuba which resulted in the death of an Italian tourist: Posada Carriles maintained that any tourists were rightful targets because their money helped prop up the Castro regime. Three years later, he was again arrested in Panama, allegedly in possession of 200 pounds of explosives and intending to blow up Fidel when he attended the Ibero-American summit in November 2000. Once more he was outsmarted by Cuban intelligence, and he and three others were seized and charged with attempted murder.

Fidel Castro was able to use both the spectre of violence perpetrated by exiles such as Posada Carriles and Bosch, as well as the new legislative measures brought in by Washington to rally the country behind him. In speech after speech, he emphasized that the world was now 'unipolar' – that there was only one superpower, which was hostile to Cuba. However, he argued, the capitalism pursued by the United States offered little hope to the developing world for economic progress or social justice. Once again, he tried to hold Cuba up as the example of what a small, independent country could achieve by resisting what he called 'the empire'. Whereas until now in the twentieth century the socialist model had acted as a counterweight to capitalism, it seemed that the world had now entered the era of 'the end of history', when the only model offered was that offered by market-led capitalism. In response, Castro stressed the moral foundations of the revolutionary regime.

An emotional reminder of the distance travelled over 30 years came in the same year of 1997, when the remains of Che Guevara were finally repatriated from Bolivia, after a joint Cuban-Argentine forensic team had identified his body, where it had remained secretly interred since 1967. Now he was reburied with great pomp in a specially built mausoleum in the city of Santa Clara, where he had won one of the most famous victories in the fight against Batista. As always, Fidel used the occasion to make a lengthy speech to the assembled crowds, declaring that Che was 'anywhere where there is a just cause to defend.' Addressing his former comrade directly, he insisted:

> Che is fighting and winning more battles than ever. Thank you, Che, for your history, your life, and your example. Thank you for coming to reinforce us in the difficult struggle in which we are engaged today to preserve the ideas for which you fought so hard ... You are a prophet for all the poor people of the world.[10]

An equally significant visitor to the island a few months later was Pope John Paul II. His visit in January 1998 raised huge expectations on all sides. Known to be staunchly anti-communist, Pope John Paul II had visited his native Poland and other countries in Eastern Europe to celebrate the fall of communism. Many of the anti-Castro zealots in Miami were convinced he would help hasten the fall of the regime in Cuba. In the event, Castro once again managed to turn the occasion to his own benefit by appearing to be a moderate leader respectful of others' spiritual beliefs. The Catholic Church did win some privileges on the island, and religious communities in general no longer faced the harassment that had taken place in the 1960s and 1970s, but the Pope's visit did not mark any great watershed in the life of most Cubans.

Another possible crisis was also turned to Castro's advantage in November 1999. This time the trigger was the plight of a five-year-old boy, Elián González. He was rescued off the Florida coast from a raft launched by his mother and her boyfriend, who had both died at sea while trying to reach the United States. The boy's future turned into a tug-of-war between the Miami anti-Castro Cubans and his father and the authorities in Cuba. The tussles over where Elián should live brought out all the old fire in Castro (perhaps reminded of similar struggles he had faced over custody for his own son almost 50 years earlier). He denounced the exiled Cubans and the u.s. administration for putting ideology above family ties, and claimed the Miami Cubans were abducting the boy against his will. It took until June 2000 for the matter to be resolved, when the boy was eventually returned to his father while a million people, with Castro naturally at their head, marched through the streets of Havana to welcome him home and celebrate another revolutionary 'triumph'.

As the Elián González saga demonstrated, even though he was by now in his seventies, Fidel Castro remained firmly in personal charge. In October 1997, the Fifth Communist Party Congress ratified him as first secretary of the party. He also continued to occupy the positions of president of the council of state, and commander-in-chief of the Cuban armed forces. The younger generation of politicians and loyal Communist party bureaucrats who perhaps thought their time had come were firmly put in their places when several of their most prominent figures were expelled from the party. In spite of the many predictions, Cuba did not go the way of Poland or East Germany, or the other Eastern European Soviet satellites. Cuba's idiosyncratic model of socialism survived because of the efficient suppression of political dissent, as well as thanks to the safety valve of exit visas. The army, still closely controlled by Raúl Castro, had been purged of potential troublemakers. Despite all they had been through, many Cubans still felt loyalty towards Fidel, as well as fear of what might happen if he were no longer in charge. He himself plainly had no thoughts of retiring. As Alfredo Guevara, his friend from his student days back in the 1940s, told me at the time: 'Fidel's not the sort of man who wants to take things easily, to go fishing and watch the world go by.'[11] But as the new millennium was to show, not even Fidel Castro could halt the march of time.

8

Time's Wingèd Chariot

By the dawn of the twenty-first century, Fidel had been in power for over 50 years. His personal influence within Cuba was still paramount. He had already ordered a reverse to the slight opening to private markets and 'self-employment'. In 2003 it once more became illegal to hold u.s. dollars, and all hard currency held by Cubans was meant to be exchanged for a new 'convertible' peso, at a charge of 10 per cent tax. These new pesos soon disparagingly became known as *chavitos*, in reference to Fidel's new international supporter, the Venezuelan president Hugo Chávez. To some extent, these changes reflected the fact that the Cuban economy had managed to survive, and not collapse entirely in the manner of the Eastern European bloc. This was due to the increasingly vital aid from Venezuela, but also to continued support from China. Trade agreements were signed with Beijing between 2001 and 2006, making the newly emerging superpower Cuba's second largest trading partner after Chávez's Venezuela. Another importance source of hard currency was the booming tourist industry. Arrivals from abroad (apart of course from the United States) grew from around 250,000 in the mid-1980s to more than two million by 2006. These tourists brought in more than u.s. $2 billion for the Cuban economy.[1]

As the 2003 reversal over the u.s. dollar showed, Fidel and many members of the inner circle who had been with the Revolution from the beginning were increasingly worried about the growing income disparities on the island. Many people who had been given education and training at the state's expense found it far more lucrative to live off dollar tips from tourists than to practise their profession. The black economy was booming, and although seldom admitted by the authorities, Havana was once more attracting foreigners looking for cheap sex. In an attempt to stimulate the revolutionary spirit of the younger generation (30 per cent of Cuba's by now 11 million population were under 21 in 2002) Fidel declared that there should be a 'Battle of Ideas' – debates at all levels of society on the continued relevance of socialism as against the globally predominant forces of capitalism. Although this debate was taken up in universities and promoted by state-backed social workers who were brought in to try to deal with the many thousands of what were euphemistically known as '*desvinculados*' (disconnected or disaffected) unemployed youngsters, the effort soon fizzled out.

This was followed by a campaign against corruption, led by the young communist newspaper *Juventud Rebelde*. These ranged from siphoning off petrol at state-run petrol stations, stealing from building sites, hospitals and medical practices, shops cheating on the amounts they sold, robbing food from tourist hotels and so on: low level misdemeanours often seen as the only way to survive. By the early years of the new millennium, the Cuban economy had stabilized, but at a far lower level than it had enjoyed thirty years earlier, and with far greater discrepancies between those either with jobs in the state sector or with foreign companies, and the millions of Cubans who had no access to any of those privileges. More disturbingly still, it was in the countryside and among the poorer educated (including a high proportion of black Cubans, who now made up a third of the total population) that these differences were most keenly felt. This created social tensions rarely seen in the earlier years of the Cuban Revolution and made the regime even shakier internally.

However, although it had appeared that Castro's was a lonely voice throughout the 1990s, internationally the following decade saw a resurgence of support and interest in the Cuban anti-imperialist and anti-capitalist stance. In the face of globalization and the dominance of the market and apparently unbridled consumerism, his constant reminder that other values were more important (however distorted these had become in Cuba over more than 40 years of Revolution) won him a fresh audience among young people and a new generation of politicians. This was particularly true in Latin America, where doubts about the benefits of 'neo-liberalism' that had been the orthodoxy in many countries throughout the 1990s led to the emergence of new governments more sympathetic to the Cuban leader's professed ideals, and what were seen as his regime's achievements in social welfare despite all the odds. His most ardent admirer was Hugo Chávez of Venezuela. Chávez, a former paratrooper who won the presidential election in 1998, had long been a supporter of Fidel Castro and his regime. He soon became his most important ally, setting up preferential deals for the supply of much-needed oil to Cuba (by 2006 this was providing more than half of Cuba's needs at prices some 40 per cent lower than the international average). President Chávez also paid the Cuban state for the use of Cuban doctors and other health experts, who were despatched in their thousands to set up health clinics in Venezuelan cities and the countryside as part of his 'Bolivarian Revolution', aimed at improving the lives of the poorer sectors of Venezuelan society. In 2004, the two leaders were also instrumental in setting up ALBA (The Bolivarian Alliance for the Peoples of Our America), intended to create free trade between its partners as an alternative to the United States Free Trade of the Americas (ALCA) initiative. At the same time, several other countries in Latin America sought closer ties with Cuba, from President Lula in Brazil to the left-wing Peronist governments in Argentina and Bolivia under President Evo Morales, another firm friend of Fidel's. These new alliances, often based on close personal ties with the Cuban leader himself, gave Castro a renewed prominence – if only on a symbolic level – as the person who had stood out against u.s. 'imperialism' for more than half a century.

The George W. Bush administration in fact stepped up its efforts to isolate the Castro regime. The Helms–Burton Bill of 1996, which established sanctions against any foreign (and not just u.s.) firms doing business with Cuba, was more regularly enforced; visits by family members to Cuba were blocked, and a 'Commission for the Assistance to a Free Cuba' team was set up. Inaugurated in 2006 with a budget of u.s. $80 million, this commission had three main priorities, according to its mission statement:

> [to] bring about a peaceful, near-term end to the dictatorship; establish democratic institutions, respect for human rights; and the rule of law; [and to] create the core institutions of a free economy.

Heading this group was the grandly termed 'Co-ordinator for the Cuban transition', Caleb McCarry. As he told me in interview: 'Our objective in Cuba is to offer our support in a respectful manner to the Cuban people in order to help them recover their freedom after 47 years of a brutal dictatorship'. As ever, Fidel Castro used this threat from outside to call for greater unity inside Cuba – and to crack down yet again on any dissent. On several occasions activists calling for political reforms were arrested and accused of being 'counter-revolutionaries' in the pay of the u.s. interests section in Havana. But the early 2000s saw a growing number of opposition figures willing to take on the regime and call for political change. The best known of these was the Varela Project. Led by Oswaldo Payá and the Christian Liberation Movement, which he helped found in 1988, the project collected more than the necessary 10,000 signatures which under the terms of the national constitution should have been enough to trigger a referendum calling for changes to legislation. These aimed to bring in freedom of association and expression, an independent press, the right to set up a wide variety of private businesses, and an amnesty for the hundreds of political prisoners they claimed were held on the island. These demands were addressed to the National Assembly, but never met with any response. Fidel himself dismissed the initiative as 'the latest brilliant idea in a series of dozens the United States has had', implying that this and all the others were inspired by a Miami 'terrorist mafia'. Undeterred, Payá and other Christian Liberation figures also called for a National Dialogue, although so far this has also fallen on deaf ears. Although Payá himself was not arrested, in March 2003, as many as 75 human rights activists were arrested and given long prison sentences.

In part, the growth of these opposition movements, as well as the open protests in the summer of 2004, were a result of the paralysis in the regime due to Fidel Castro's increasing health problems. Not only the general direction of government, but also many day-to-day decisions still depended almost exclusively on him. In 2001 he fainted from the heat while giving one of his marathon speeches. Immediately there was intense speculation about who might succeed him, and if the Revolution would take a different path once he was no longer in charge. As on previous occasions, while the faithful were asserting that the transition to another generation would be accomplished without traumas because all the institutions of government were based on principles rather than personalities, Castro soon moved to assert his authority again. He sacked several younger figures in the administration whom he saw as becoming too prominent, and brought in stricter controls on the use of dollars, private markets and self-employment.

Another fall in October 2004, when he broke a kneecap and his arm, confirmed Fidel's frailty. But it was at the end of July 2006 that his grip on power was finally broken. As a result of a mismanaged stomach operation for diverticulitis, he was left in such a weak condition that he handed over the running of government to his younger brother Raúl (who by now was 75 years old). Over the following months it became clear that the 80-year-old Fidel was never likely to recover his former energy and robust health, although he was well enough to comment: 'I'm really happy to reach 80. I never expected it, not least having a neighbour – the greatest power in the world – trying to kill me every day.'

Immediate measures were taken to ensure a smooth transfer of power. Raúl was appointed acting president until his position could be ratified by the National Assembly. In the run-up to a meeting of the National Assembly in February 2008, Fidel Castro was yet again elected as the representative for Santiago de Cuba. However, he soon sent a letter stressing that he did not wish to be put forward for election to any official positions. 'I will not aspire to nor accept – I repeat, I will not aspire to or accept – the post of President of the Council of State and Commander in Chief', he wrote, effectively announcing his retirement from public affairs after close to five decades in power. In 2011 this process was completed when he stepped down as leader of the Communist Party of Cuba.

His brother Raúl replaced him in this post, and all the others. For more than half a century, the two brothers complemented each other very successfully. Fidel has always seen himself as the visionary, the 'maximum leader', with Raúl filling in behind. The elder brother is the man who organizes and is concerned with the details that can make the vision become a reality, or try to prevent it turning into a nightmare. There is little doubt that Raúl was always the more convinced communist, apparently following a 1953 tour of Europe that took him not only to Vienna, then controlled by the Soviets, but to Romania, Hungary and Czechoslovakia. This ideological conviction was also reinforced by a lack of knowledge of the 'colossus of the north', the United States. Over many years he had

Handing over power to Raúl, 2008.

only visited it once, and then for less than 24 hours, during a trip to Texas to talk to his brother at Houston airport.

According to many commentators, it has also been Raúl who has kept the Castro family together. He has smoothed over the situation with Fidel's divorced first wife, Mirta Díaz-Balart, and also with Juanita. Naty Revuelta's daughter, Alina Fernández, singled him out as being kind to her, and much more human than her distant father. Over the years, Raúl has kept very quiet about any private ambitions he may have had to replace his brother at the head of government. From the outset, he never challenged his brother's right to be in charge. After the two brothers returned to Cuba in 1956, he was content to play a subordinate role in the guerrilla struggle. He proved to be an able commander in the war when his brother put him in charge of one of the columns with the responsibility for bringing the fight down out of the mountains in the east of the country. It was then that his capacity as an organizer came into its own. He kept a detailed diary of his time in the mountains, claiming he was able to expand the original group of some 53 men into more than a thousand in less than a year. According to Brian Latell, 'he created an elaborate revolutionary administration that in many ways would be the model for the new regime in Havana.'[2]

When the rebels succeeded in ousting Batista at the beginning of 1959, Raúl was given the task, along with Che Guevara, of organizing the new revolutionary army. In the process, they both earned the reputation of being the 'hard men' of the Revolution: the ones who were in charge of signing and carrying out death warrants on Batista torturers and corrupt followers. Raúl was keenly in favour of closer links with the Soviet Union. From the mid-1960s onward, he ensured that all military officers went there for training: an obvious necessity, as their equipment was by now coming from the USSR and its allies. In the 1970s it was Raúl who was most stridently opposed to what was termed 'ideological diversionism', denouncing anyone and everyone who did not share the regime's views, and in particular the homosexual community. Most importantly, he succeeded handsomely in organizing the new armed forces, and ever since has managed to secure their loyalty to the regime and to Fidel himself. There has never been any indication that he has tried to use this position to undermine, still much less replace his brother. Raúl is widely seen to have kept the armed forces quiet and loyal by being someone who promoted people on merit, and showed sufficient concern for them to feel personally loyal to him. Of course, he has also seen to it that their privileges and rewards have been substantial. His most difficult moment with the armed forces came in 1989, with the trial and execution of General Arnaldo Ochoa, who had been his close friend and confidant since the days in the sierra.

Raúl's relationship with Fidel survived this crisis, and it was due to the closeness of their bond that despite the Ochoa incident the armed forces were given a leading role in promoting Cuba's effort to attract foreign tourists, and on many other joint ventures. Although since the 1960s it had been Raúl who was Fidel's chief point of contact with the Soviet Union (he had gone to Moscow in 1962 to thrash out the details of the missile deal with Khrushchev, and returned there after their withdrawal to remonstrate with the Soviet authorities), it was to his brother that Fidel often turned in the particularly harsh period following the Soviet withdrawal in the early 1990s.

After taking over from Fidel as acting president of Cuba in 2006, Raúl at first proceeded cautiously, as if still looking over his shoulder to see if his brother approved. He stressed continuity, and many of the replacements he made, including that of a new vice-president (the 76-year-old Machado Ventura), were from among the gerontocracy that had fought in the Revolution against Batista. He gradually replaced high-ranking members of the government who were closely linked to his brother, such as long-standing Minister of Foreign Affairs Felipe Pérez Roque or economics supremo Carlos Lage, with others he considered owed him more loyalty. His attempts to improve the economy have been based on 'efficiency' and the elimination of bureaucracy, without attempting any more fundamental overhaul of the system. He has brought in some popular measures: for example, the right to have mobile phones or – if they have enough dollars – to stay in the tourist hotels that have sprung up over the past two decades but were previously off limits to ordinary Cubans. Internationally, Raúl has also continued with his brother's policies: although he declared himself willing to discuss 'anything and everything' with Washington, he has made little effort, in public at least, to bring any real change to relations between the two countries. Although the arrival of President Obama in 2008 raised hopes that there might be a relaxation of the u.s. trade embargo, the State Department dismissed Raúl's rule as 'dictatorship-lite' and declared that only a real transition towards 'free and fair' elections with competing political parties would lead to a re-consideration of policy towards Cuba.

By 2010, however, it was plain that Raúl felt in a strong enough position to bring in economic and political changes that were radically different from those espoused by his brother. In December 2010 he declared 'Either we rectify or the time to continue teetering on the edge of the precipice is over, and we fall'.[3] This new process of 'rectification' was outlined in detail at the Sixth Congress of the Communist Party of Cuba (which had been delayed since 2002). In the run-up to the April 2011 Congress, Raúl announced a massive lay off of up to half a million employees in the state sector, although the deep unease this announcement created led him to row back on exactly when these dismissals would take place. This hesitant approach led many observers to believe that few drastic measures would be proposed at the Congress, but in fact the sessions saw the most far-reaching changes envisaged for many years. Although in the past, when Fidel was in charge, Raúl had consistently argued for a centralized, state-run economy, now he sought (and received) approval for proposals that would greatly reduce the role of the state in the economy. The huge lay offs are to be compensated by the legalization of some 180 occupations, from clowns to carpenters, hairdressers to private transport companies. More land was promised for private farmers. And for the first time since the Revolution, people running businesses will be officially permitted to take on employees who are not family members. Cubans are also to be allowed to buy and sell houses, cars, and other goods, while rules on obtaining passports and travelling abroad are also to be relaxed. Since these measures are designed to increase personal finances, the ration book that has supplied basic needs since the 1960s is also to be phased out. The main thrust of these measures is to cut government spending in order to reduce the massive deficit. The state will still be the main economic force in the economy, and the communist party will continue to impose its authoritarian rule. Raúl's gamble appears to be that Cuba in the second decade of the twenty-first century can adopt the kind of mixture of capitalism and one party rule that is being followed in China and Vietnam. He appears to be gambling on the idea that by keeping strict control over the armed forces and the communist party, this hybrid can produce results that will generate enough economic growth to keep the majority of Cubans happy.

Fidel's fading health (he was almost 85 when the congress was held) meant that he did not sit through the debates on Raúl's radical proposals. However, he did appear at the final session, and endorsed the work of the Congress. In fact, since his illness and retirement from active politics, he has been careful to confine his observations and comments to international affairs, and to make it plain that it is Raúl in charge domestically. And yet there remains a strong sense in Cuba that he will continue to cast his shadow over his younger brother until what many people call the 'biological solution' occurs. In Spain, it was not until that other Galician caudillo, Francisco Franco, died after almost 40 years as head of state that any real change could take place. The same is likely to prove true in Cuba.

Conclusion: The Great Survivor

As early as 1953, Fidel Castro was calling on history to be his judge. Now that he is finally retired from any position of power in Cuba, the time has come for at least a preliminary verdict on his successes and failures. The self-belief evident from that defence speech in 1953 has been his most overwhelming personal trait. That is what took him from being a student leader in Havana to the leader of the political opposition against the Batista dictatorship. It propelled him into the guerrilla adventure in the mountains, and enabled his hugely outnumbered band of rebels to inflict defeat on a much more powerful and better-trained adversary. And this victory was achieved in only two years. After coming to power in 1959, Fidel then set about a top-to-bottom revolutionary re-ordering of Cuban society. He was determined to modernize the Cuban economy, bring about much greater social justice in a very unequal society, and to carry the people with him, at times almost entirely by force of will.

Internationally, possibly the Cuban leader's greatest success has been the reputation he gained for standing up defiantly to American imperialism. In the rest of Latin America and in many Third World countries in Africa and Asia, he was seen as the David against a brutal Goliath, which repeatedly flaunted international law and its own rhetoric to impose its world view on other less powerful countries. This image had in fact first been used by the nineteenth-century Cuban liberation hero José Martí, who wrote of his years in exile in the United States: 'I have lived in the bowels of the monster and know him well, and my sling is David's.'[1] This myth was still powerful for Castro, although never explicitly referred to.

Beyond his own continent, he was regarded, especially in the 1970s and 1980s, as offering support to national liberation movements and newly independent countries in Africa. He was instrumental in trying to create new alignments that could exist as a counterbalance to the 'First World' or the 'North'. However, this position as the 'leader of the Non-Aligned Movement' was severely compromised at the 1973 summit meeting of the group in Algiers, when he spoke of the USSR as the 'natural ally' of the developing world. Whatever Castro's rhetoric about a position independent of the two superpowers, he was increasingly seen – in the United States of course, but also by other emerging nations – as being part of one camp.

After the collapse of the Soviet Union and its European allies, many analysts predicted the imminent demise of the Castro regime. The reasons this did not happen owe something to the fact that Fidel was still an inspiring figure within Cuba. But they are much more due to the pursuit of mainly non-socialist efforts to obtain foreign currency needed to stay afloat: tourism (in 2008, some 2.4 million tourists brought in some U.S. $3 billion), attempts to garner the massive inflow of dollar remittances from the million or more Cubans living in the United States, plus renewed calls for the Cuban people to accept further sacrifices, food rationing, poor housing, and the lack of possibilities to buy consumer goods. The United States has helped in this sense, especially when the hard-line approach towards trade with the island won out during the Bush administrations, but also under Bill Clinton. Whereas some in Washington argued that opening Cuba to trade with the United States would rapidly lead to demands for more freedom, the opposite view won out: 'Why should we reward a dictator who has been oppressing his people for forty years?', as I was told by a high-ranking member of the U.S.-interests section in Havana at the time. It is only since Barack Obama became president at the start of 2009 that there has been some relaxation of these measures, with Cuban-Americans allowed once more to travel to visit relatives on the island, and to send dollars officially.

But what kind of society is it that Fidel Castro has played such a central role in creating? Over 50 years on from the Revolution, it can hardly be said to be 'socialist'. The state has certainly been used to promote equality. There is schooling for everyone without hierarchies, making it very different from Fidel's own childhood. Health care has been vastly improved, with most medicines available to everyone, although party membership has distorted access to hospitals and other medical centres. But although many doctors and nurses come through the education system, they often find that the only work for them is in other countries, where they are used as 'solidarity' pawns for their expertise. In health matters as elsewhere, the presence of the state can become oppressive. This is the case with the HIV/AIDS problem. When the first cases began to appear in the mid-1980s, the response of the Cuban government was to shut all HIV sufferers away so that they would not spread the disease. Blood tests for signs of the illness were made compulsory in every workplace. Measures such as these led to criticism internationally that individuals were being punished on the basis of their possible future behaviour, but the Castro regime argues that social responsibility is more important than individual rights.

There is little worker control over production: there may be several thousand state-run enterprises, but few ordinary Cubans feel that these in any sense 'belong' to them. As in the Soviet Union, society in Cuba is divided in two. There are those who follow the accepted line: membership of the communist party, a position of responsibility in one of the state concerns (not merely in industry, but also in the academic or scientific spheres). These people enjoy a relatively privileged position. They can buy more goods, are better housed, earn more money, and are allowed to travel outside Cuba. Their loyalty to the regime is rewarded, and as long as they continue to enjoy these benefits, they will not rock the boat in any way. This of course applies even more to members of the Cuban armed forces, who have taken advantage of being given control over the tourist industry and many building projects, and have been able to consolidate a position of privilege that is denied to most other sectors of the population.

On the other hand, there are millions of Cubans who do not have access to these privileges. The older generation has known nothing but sacrifice and shortages. While a fair proportion still support Fidel and his associates, they are above all concerned with getting by, trying to find ways to get the dollars that make all the difference, trying to keep families together in often appalling housing conditions. The younger generation seems almost entirely apolitical. As one young man joked to me, in an echo of Che Guevara's apparent gaffe that led to him becoming head of Cuba's national bank: 'we're not *comunistas* any more, we're *consumistas*'. Unfortunately, they feel there is little for them to consume in today's Cuba, and they also suffer from a lack of work opportunities, as well as resentment that it is so hard for them to travel outside the island (and in many cases, to move freely within it). The idea of socialist solidarity is conspicuously lacking in Cuba after over 50 years of revolution: it is the individual and then the family that matter above all. Their attitude to the state is no more trusting than anywhere else in Latin America, where repression, corruption and a failure to keep promises have often led ordinary citizens to seek to have as little to do with it as possible.

One of the main goals of the 1959 Revolution was to achieve economic independence after centuries as a colony of Spain, and decades in the twentieth century when the economy depended almost entirely on trade with the United States and investment from there. The paradox lies in the fact that Cuba under Castro never succeeded in generating enough of an economic surplus to be able to finance its modernization in any independent fashion. All too soon, its dependency on the United States turned into a similarly asymmetrical one with the Soviet Union, with the result that national industry remained largely undeveloped. When Cuba was thrown on its own resources in the 1990s, there was a scramble to earn hard currency by any means – from tourism, to the sale of the stock of American cars from the Batista era – but once again with little or no investment that might increase the island's self-sufficiency. Even in the last decade, Cuba has had to import more than two-thirds of its food needs.[2] Yet another paradox is that an estimated U.S. $500 million worth of that food has been imported from the United States, making Cuba's fifth most important trade partner, in spite of the embargo. And the partnership that has thrown the Revolution a lifeline since the year 2000 – the close relationship with President Hugo Chávez and his 'Bolivarian Revolution' in Venezuela – involves a fresh dependency on another country. However well disposed that country may be at present, it means that the solutions to Cuba's problems of energy needs, foreign currency and investment (Venezuela's input into the Cuban economy was put at more than U.S. $3 billion in 2009) are at the mercy of political developments in a third country, rather than being in its own hands.

President Chávez's support for Cuba is in large part due to his respect, not to say adoration, of Fidel himself. While the charisma of the Cuban leader is undeniable, over the years it has increasingly become a danger for any real democracy in Cuba. It is often said triumphantly that Fidel Castro has seen ten U.S. presidents come and go, as if this were a recommendation. But it hardly seems to be a sign of the Cuban people having any choice to replace the person governing them, whatever his outstanding personal qualities. If one of the main aims of the Revolution was to free the talents and capabilities of millions of Cubans who had been kept down by

Meeting Pope Benedict XIV, March 2012.

colonial repression and then by even more repressive home-grown dictatorships, why has there been no one seen to be worthy to take over from the 'maximum leader' to take the process on another stage? Over the past five decades, there have been several moments when a leader truly concerned with the progress of his people might have stepped down: in 1970, after the failure to reach the ten million tons sugar harvest, which Fidel himself had made a life-or-death issue. In 1975–6, when the Revolution was properly institutionalized, and a new constitution drawn up – could Fidel not have considered his job done at that point, and taken a more background role, making the presidency the position of an elder statesman removed from the day-to-day running of the country? What about 1980, when the massive Mariel boatlift showed just how unpopular the regime he had created had become? Or together with the other 'socialist' leaders in the early 1990s, as an admission of the comprehensive failure of his policies, and the direction he had taken by allying his regime so closely with the Soviet Union? Yet each new twist in the historical developments of recent years has seen Fidel even more determined to carry on, as if the whole of Cuba had to go along with him while he worked out his response to circumstances. It was only in December 2007, when due to failing health he declined to be made leader of the National Assembly yet again, that he wrote, without the slightest trace of irony, that he had no wish 'to obstruct the rise of younger persons.'

For many years, his was virtually the only voice heard announcing policy decisions in Cuba. One of the most depressing aspects of life in Cuba was to go and listen to Fidel speaking. Particularly as he grew older, he would ramble on from subject to subject, far from the question he was supposedly addressing, while nobody else was allowed to say a word, to challenge anything he said, or to get up and leave. Power in Cuba under Fidel has never been shared by more than a tight handful of trusted allies – many of whom have been 'purged' at different stages along the way. This has

"CUBA POSTCASTRO"

A defiant view of Cuba after Castro: a poster of 2011.

hardly ever been as drastic as the Stalinist purges in the Soviet Union, but imprisonment, exile and occasionally execution (as with the Ochoa brothers, who were at the very apex of the power structure), have been used throughout the almost 50 years of Castro's rule to deal with any possible dissent. And as Fidel and his associates have aged, they have increasingly resisted any attempts by younger figures to take over. Several generations of younger leaders, encouraged to rise through the ranks of the communist party, have found their careers suddenly truncated when they took too independent a line or were seen to be a potential threat. This process appears to have continued under Raúl Castro, who in 2010 removed several younger ministers in favour of older, more trusted colleagues.

Fidel Castro is probably more surprised than anyone that his final days have seen him slowly fading out of the picture. Always one to cast himself in a heroic mould, botched medical operations and a slow decline hardly fitted in with the mythical proportions of the death of Che Guevara or his companions in the guerrilla struggle in the Sierra Maestra. It must have been even more painful to watch from the sidelines as his younger brother cautiously dismantled much of the idiosyncratic regime he himself did so much to fashion over five decades. Fidel Castro's life has been a constant challenge to History; the last thing he could have envisaged was that it might simply ignore him.

References

Preface

1 Author interview.
2 Brian Latell, *After Fidel* (New York, 2002), p. 20.
3 Fidel Castro, with Ignacio Ramonet, *My Life: A Spoken Autobiography* (London, 2007).

1 Down on the Farm

1 Castro, *My Life*, p. 25.
2 Richard Gott, *Cuba: A New History* (New Haven, CT, 2004), p. 91.
3 Hugh Thomas, *Cuba or the Pursuit of Freedom* (London, 1971), p. 431.
4 Castro, *My Life*, p. 27.
5 Tad Szulc, *Fidel: A Critical Portrait* (London, 1986), p. 43.
6 George Galloway, *Fidel Castro Handbook* (London, 2006) p. 14.
7 For many years, there was considerable argument as to whether in fact Fidel Castro was born in 1926 or 1927, until Castro himself finally confirmed the earlier date. Interestingly, there has been similar confusion over the correct birth date of one of the other iconic figures of the Cuban Revolution, the Argentine Ernesto 'Che' Guevara. As some observers have noted, this confusion only serves to increase the aura of the two men as mythical heroes.
8 See Nick Caistor, *Che Guevara: A Life* (Oxford, 2009), p. 11.
9 Castro, *My Life*, p. 37.
10 Ibid., p. 31.
11 Frei Betto, *Fidel y la Religión*, Oficina de Publicaciones del Consejo de

Esrado (Havana, 1985), p. 41.

12 Deborah Shnookal and Pedro Alvarez Tabío, eds, *Fidel: My Early Years* (Melbourne and New York, 2005), p. 23.

13 Patrick Symmes, *The Boys from Dolores: Fidel Castro's Classmates from Revolution to Exile* (London 2007), pp. 336–7.

14 Ann Louise Bardach, *Cuba Confidential: The Extraordinary Tragedy of Cuba, its Revolution and its Exiles* (London, 2004), p. 60.

15 Ann Louise Bardach, *Without Fidel* (New York, 2009), p. 87.

16 Castro, *My Life*, p. 80.

17 Symmes, *The Boys from Dolores*, p. 58.

18 Castro, *My Life*, p. 504.

2 Defying the Dictator

1 Author interview.

2 Richard Gott, *Cuba: A New History*, pp. 135–41.

3 Lionel Martin, *The Early Fidel: Roots of Castro's Communism* (Secaucus, NJ, 1978), p. 30.

4 Ibid., p. 45.

5 Ibid., p. 98.

6 Ibid., p. 98.

7 Ibid., p. 101.

8 Sheldon B. Liss, *Roots of Revolution: Radical Thought in Cuba* (Lincoln, NE, 1987), p. 17.

9 Author interview.

10 Szulc, *Fidel: A Critical Portrait*, p. 212.

11 Martin, *The Early Fidel*, p. 140.

12 When I asked the British Marxist historian if he thought history would 'absolve' Fidel Castro, he immediately objected to this usual translation as being too religious in tone. He preferred the more legally precise 'acquit': he also thought history would look kindly on the Cuban leader.

13 Tomás Borge, *Face to Face with Fidel Castro* (Melbourne, 1992), p. 42.

14 Martin, *The Early Fidel*, p. 151.

15 Luis Conte Agüero, ed., *The Prison Letters of Fidel Castro* (New York, 2007), pp. 53–4.

16 Ibid., p. 61.

17 Martin, *The Early Fidel*, p. 167.

18 Caistor, *Che Guevara: A Life*, p. 39.

19 Sebastian Balfour, *Castro: Profiles in Power* (Harlow, 2009), p. 43.

3 Making the Revolution

1 Jean-Paul Sartre, *Sartre on Cuba* (Westport, CT, 1974), p. 17.

2 Quoted in Jon Lee Anderson, *Che Guevara: A Revolutionary Life* (London, 1997), p. 245.

3 Bardach, *Cuba Confidential*, p. 15.

4 Caistor, *Che Guevara: A Life*, p. 51.

5 Castro, *My Life*, p. 193.

6 Author interview.

7 Szulc, *Fidel: A Critical Portrait*, p. 375.

8 Martin, *The Early Fidel*, p. 234.

9 Dayan Jayatilleka, *Fidel's Ethics of Violence: The Moral Dimension of the Political Thought of Fidel Castro* (London, 2007), p. 74.

10 Ibid., p. 84.

11 Castro, *My Life*, p. 220.

12 Jean Stubbs, *Cuba: The Test of Time* (London, 1989), p. 33.

13 Castro, *My Life*, pp. 101–2.

14 Liss, *Roots of Revolution*, p. 24.

4 Missiles and Marxism

1 Szulc, *Fidel: A Critical Portrait*, p. 451.

2 Ibid., p. 384.

3 Author interview.

4 Castro, *My Life*, p. 278.

5 Quoted in Acosta.

6 Maurice Halperin, *The Rise and Decline of Fidel Castro*, pp. 287–97.

7 René Dumont, *Is Cuba Socialist?* (New York, 1974), p. 75.

8 Gott, *Cuba: A New History*, p. 214.

9 Author interview.

10 Anderson, *Che Guevara: A Revolutionary Life*, p. 397.

11 Castro, *My Life*, p. 300.

12 Ibid., pp. 703–4.

13 Anderson, *Che Guevara: A Revolutionary Life*, p. 741.

14 Szulc, *Fidel: A Critical Portrait*, p. 468.

15 Bardach, *Cuba Confidential*, p. 173.

16 Szulc, *Fidel: A Critical Portrait*, pp. 491–2.

17 Balfour, *Castro: Profiles in Power*, p. 3.

5 Revolution and the State

1 Castro, *My Life*, pp. 579–80.

2 Quoted in 'Castro's Speech to Intellectuals on 30 June 61', at lanic.utexas.edu (accessed 6 November 2012).

3 Samuel Farber, *Cuba Since the Revolution of 1959* (Chicago, IL, 2011), p. 21.

4 See Dumont, *Is Cuba Socialist?*, p. 111. In particular, his description of Castro as someone who 'follows his own ideas, convinced that they are the best. Thus he assumes unchecked personal power, and this fosters a courtier-like approach in those around him. When he throws his beret on the ground and flies into one of his rages, everybody quakes and fears reprisals.'

5 Gerald Martin, *Gabriel García Márquez: A Life* (London, 2008), p. 183.

6 Ibid., p. 246.

7 Ibid., pp. 397–8.

8 Balfour, *Castro: Profiles in Power*, p. 92.

9 Ibid., p. 93.

10 Stubbs, *Cuba: The Test of Time*, p. 18.

11 Szulc, *Fidel: A Critical Portrait*, p. 511.

12 Martin, *Gabriel García Márquez: A Life*, p. 185.

13 Author interview.

14 Sartre, *Sartre on Cuba*, p. 15.

15 Shnookal and Alvarez Tabío, *Fidel: My Early Years*, p. 18.

16 Liss, *Roots of Revolution*, p. 42.

6 Losing the Plot

1 Castro, *My Life*, p. 405.
2 See Gott, *Cuba: A New History*, pp. 266–9.
3 See Alina Fernández Revuelta, *Castro's Daughter: An Exile's Memory of Cuba*, (New York, 1999).
4 Bardach, *Without Fidel*, p. 36.
5 Ibid., p. 65.
6 Author interview.
7 Stubbs, *Cuba: The Test of Time*, p. 8.
8 Quoted in Balfour, *Castro: Profiles in Power*, p. 136.
9 Castro, *My Life*, p. 360.
10 Balfour, *Castro: Profiles in Power*, p. 151.
11 Gott, *Cuba: A New History*, pp. 279–86.
12 Author interview.
13 *Granma International*, 14 July 1989.

7 The Special Period

1 Balfour, *Castro: Profiles in Power*, p. 154.
2 Author interview.
3 Balfour, *Castro: Profiles in Power*, p. 153.
4 Gott, *Cuba: A New History*, pp. 303–4.
5 Bardach, *Without Fidel*, p. 111.
6 Ibid., p. 136.
7 *La Vanguardia*, 16 August 2006.
8 *Granma International*, 11 June 2009.
9 Bardach, *Without Fidel*, p. 134.
10 Caistor, *Che Guevara: A Life*, p. 141.
11 Author interview.

8 Time's Wingèd Chariot

1 Balfour, *Castro: Profiles in Power,* p. 171.
2 Latell, *After Fidel,* p. 125.
3 Farber, *Cuba Since the Revolution of 1959,* p. 277.

Conclusion: The Great Survivor

1 Antoni Kapcia, *Cuba in Revolution: A History Since the Fifties* (London, 2008), p. 104.
2 Bardach, *Without Fidel,* p. 268.

Select Bibliography

Anderson, Jon Lee, *Che Guevara: A Revolutionary Life* (London, 1997)

Balfour, Sebastian, *Castro: Profiles in Power* (Harlow, 2009)

Bardach, Ann Louise, *Cuba Confidential: The Extraordinary Tragedy of Cuba, its Revolution and its Exiles* (London, 2004)

——, *Without Fidel* (New York, 2009)

Bethell, Leslie, ed., *Cuba: A Short History* (Cambridge, 1993)

Betto, Frei, *Fidel y la religión*, Oficina de publicaciones del Consejo de Estado (Havana, 1985)

Borge, Tomás, *Face to Face with Fidel Castro: A Conversation with Tomás Borge* (Melbourne, 1993)

Caistor, Nick, *Che Guevara: A Life* (Oxford, 2009)

Castro, Fidel, with Ignacio Ramonet, *My Life: A Spoken Autobiography* (London, 2007)

Conte Agüero, Luis, ed., *The Prison Letters of Fidel Castro* (New York, 2007)

Debray, Régis, *Praised Be Our Lords: The Autobiography* (London, 2007)

Dumont, René, *Is Cuba Socialist?* (New York, 1974)

Escalante, Fabián, *Executive Action: 638 Ways to Kill Fidel Castro* (Melbourne, 2006)

Farber, Samuel, *Cuba Since the Revolution of 1959: A Critical Assessment* (Chicago, IL, 2011)

Fernández Revuelta, Alina, *Castro's Daughter: An Exile's Memory of Cuba* (New York, 1999)

Franqui, Carlos, *Family Portrait with Fidel: A Memoir* (London, 1983)

Galloway, George, *Fidel Castro Handbook* (London, 2006)

Gott, Richard, *Cuba: A New History* (New Haven, CT, 2004)

Halperin, Maurice, *The Rise and Decline of Fidel Castro: An Essay in Contemporary History* (London, 1972)

Jayatilleka, Dayan, *Fidel's Ethics of Violence: The Moral Dimension of the Political Thought of Fidel Castro* (London, 2007)

Kapcia, Antoni, *Cuba in Revolution: A History Since the Fifties* (London, 2008)

Karol, K. S., *Guerrillas in Power: The Course of the Cuban Revolution* (New York, 1970)

Lambie, George, *The Cuban Revolution in the 21st Century* (London, 2010)

Latell, Brian, *After Fidel* (New York, 2002)

Liss, Sheldon B., *Roots of Revolution: Radical Thought in Cuba* (Lincoln, NE, 1987)

Lumsden, Ian, *Machos, Maricones, and Gays: Cuba and Homosexuality* (Philadelphia, PA, 1996)

Marshall, Peter, *Cuba Libre: Breaking the Chains?* (London, 1987)

Martin, Gerald, *Gabriel García Márquez: A Life* (London, 2008)

Martin, Lionel, *The Early Fidel: Roots of Castro's Communism* (Secaucus, NJ, 1978)

Quirk, Robert E., *Fidel Castro* (New York, 1993)

Ritter, Archibald R. M., ed., *The Cuban Economy* (Pittsburgh, PA, 2004)

Ruffin, Patricia, *Capitalism and Socialism in Cuba: A Study of Dependency, Development and Underdevelopment* (London, 1990)

Saney, Isaac, *Cuba: A Revolution in Motion* (London, 2003)

Sartre, Jean-Paul, *Sartre on Cuba* (Westport, CT, 1974)

Shnookal, Deborah, and Pedro Alvarez Tabío, eds, *Fidel: My Early Years* (Melbourne and New York, 2005)

Symmes, Patrick, *The Boys from Dolores: Fidel Castro's Classmates from Revolution to Exile* (London, 2007)

Szulc, Tad, *Fidel: A Critical Portrait* (London, 1986)

Timerman, Jacobo, *Cuba: A Journey* (New York, 1990)

Turton, Peter, *José Martí: Architect of Cuba's Freedom* (London, 1986)

Acknowledgements

I would like to thank Julio Etchart and Liba Taylor; my BBC producer Linda Pressly for her patience; and Amanda Hopkinson for her support, as always.

Photo Acknowledgements

The author and publishers wish to express their thanks to the following sources of illustrative material and/or permission to reproduce it.

Photos courtesy of the author: pp. 13, 29, 45, 101, 144 (with thanks to Alex); Ocean Press: pp. 16, 19, 23; Prensa Latina: pp. 27, 37, 67; Wisconsin Historical Society (Dicky Chapelle): pp. 46, 50; Panos Pictures: pp. 6 (Miller), 114 (Taylor); Salas brothers: pp. 59, 61, 74, 77; U.S. Defense Department: p. 69; Julio Etchart (Julio@julioetchart.com): p. 111; Emilito: p. 132; photo Getty Images: p. 142.